CREATIVE BUSINESS

FT Prentice Hall
FINANCIAL TIMES

CREATIVE BUSINESS

The making of addictive stories

PAUL NERO

NEETA PATEL

FT Prentice Hall
FINANCIAL TIMES

An imprint of **Pearson Education**

Harlow, England • London • New York • Boston • San Francisco • Toronto
Sydney • Tokyo • Singapore • Hong Kong • Seoul • Taipei • New Delhi
Cape Town • Madrid • Mexico City • Amsterdam • Munich • Paris • Milan

PEARSON EDUCATION LIMITED

Head Office:
Edinburgh Gate
Harlow CM20 2JE
Tel: +44 (0)1279 623623
Fax: +44 (0)1279 431059

London Office:
128 Long Acre
London WC2E 9AN
Tel: +44 (0)20 7447 2000
Fax: +44 (0)20 7447 2170
Website: www.business-minds.com

First published in Great Britain in 2003

© Pearson Education Limited 2003

The right of Paul Nero and Neeta Patel to be identified as authors of this work has been asserted by them in accordance with the Copyright, Designs and Patents Act 1988.

ISBN: 0 273 65671 6

British Library Cataloguing in Publication Data
A CIP catalogue record for this book can be obtained from the British Library.

10 9 8 7 6 5 4 3 2 1

Typeset by Pantek Arts Ltd, Maidstone, Kent
Printed and bound in Great Britain by Henry Ling Ltd, Dorchester

The publishers' policy is to use paper manufactured from sustainable forests.

ACKNOWLEDGEMENTS

An awful lot of evenings in front of the television, nights at the cinema and days filled listening to music have gone into the production of this book. So have some serious thinking and much discussion with practitioners of creative businesses. Those with whom we spoke had great stories to tell, and we trust we have transferred their insights faithfully.

The book was conceived as dotcom mania spluttered its dying breath, and integration of new media businesses with older, wiser parents intensified. Consensus about the future among our contributors was rare, and everyone had a new perspective to offer. We hope the stories that follow provide an entertaining and informative read.

Our grateful thanks to those people who agreed to be interviewed and gave freely of their time – Andy Anson and David Brook at Channel 4, Ralph Ardill at Imagination, Linda Aspey of Aspey Associates, Professor Patrick Barwise at London Business School, John Conway, Richard Fell and Ashley Highfield at the BBC, Simon Cooper at GWR, John Cummings at Hawkpoint Partners, Greg Delaney at advertising agency Delaney Lund Knox Warren, Andy Harries at Granada Television, David Docherty at Telewest, James Harding at the *Financial Times*, Professor Clive Holtham of the Cass Business School, City University, John Hollar at Pearson Broadband, Jonathan Morris, Brendan Nelson, Dame Marjorie Scardino at Pearson plc, Simon Terrington and Richard Burnett at media consultancy Human Capital, and Theresa Wise at Accenture. Tom Hazledine knocked out transcripts, checked out facts and pointed out the perspective of youth, while Paul Waddington kindly gave the manuscript the once-over and defended art-house buffs.

We would also like to record our appreciation of Peter Martin who, at the time we interviewed him for this book, was deputy editor of the *Financial Times*. Peter had also been our colleague at FT.com: an outstanding man with an incisive, creative mind, a ready wit and many kindly words. Shortly before this book went to print, Peter died. He was a whirlwind, and we can't believe he's gone.

We also extend our gratitude to publisher Rachael Stock at Pearson Education for having faith in the concept, even when ours faltered, returning us to a positive outlook in the finest traditions of publishing in a West End bar.

Finally, an apology for any mistakes or misrepresentations that may have inadvertently escaped our notice and made it to print – and to those around us who have suffered many months of grumbling, whining and gnashing of teeth as these words finally came together. Thank you all.

Paul Nero
Neeta Patel

London
September 2002

CONTENTS

PROLOGUE: THE WORLD OF ADDICTIVE STORIES

1

'A great story is like an iceberg.
One-eighth is above the surface; the other seven-eights is below.'

Ernest Hemingway

It's morning. Dreams are broken, and your daily story starts. With the radio, breakfast TV, perhaps a newspaper, and a quick check of a few websites. Everyone who has a story to tell – or something to sell – wants to get to you the minute you wake, and then again throughout the day. A content overdose. Morning, noon and night, in many forms, across many media. Today, wherever we go, whatever we do, as an audience we're consuming content endlessly. If we go back for more, that – in the old dotcom phraseology – is 'sticky'. And unpleasant though it sounds, that's a very good thing. It's wicked in fact (that's good too).

Sticky content is addictive content, luring users from one place to the next, with the promise of bigger, better, purer fixes.

Sticky content is addictive content, luring users from one place to the next, with the promise of bigger, better, purer fixes. When stories catch fire and become hits, audiences are measured in millions. Millions of people, generating millions of dollars. All from a sticky story of addictive content. That which transfers across media. And hangs around.

STICKY STORIES OF OLD

When Granada Television developed a new popular drama in 1960, they expected a short run, perhaps a second series, by which time the audience would be consumed with other stories. In 2001, *Coronation Street* celebrated 40 years on British television, and more than 12 million people still tune in four nights a week. In addition to its television roots, it earns a tidy living from books, videos and format rights. On the Web, addicts can find plot and character backgrounds, quizzes and a chance to keep up to date with storylines. Serial drama is a story format that, when it engages with its audience, endures and transfers, telling new parts of its story in different media.

All this for a straightforward narrative drama, a short play with commercial breaks. A form that interactive technology was meant to have killed off. Soap operas the world over are not only not dead. Most are not even ill. They thrive, forming stronger foundations within television schedules.

While some may last for five years, others for ten, the best reinvent themselves and look like they could go on forever. Unless they are replaced with bigger stories, newer hits, which keep audiences coming back for more.

Elvis Presley was a rock and roller. He sang, played guitar, wiggled his hips and, in doing so, created a fan base that keeps on rocking today. Unlike flash-in-the-pan, one-hit wonders, he keeps selling millions of records almost 50 years after 'Heartbreak Hotel' made him a star. An executive at RCA Records is still responsible for managing his image. And remember, despite what you may read in the papers, this is a man who is dead.

Elvis was a story, and the story lives on. His Graceland home, now a tourist destination, attracts more people under the age of 25 than it did when the pearly gates were first flung open. An Internet search flushes out hundreds of thousands of links into a world of the king one never knew – and probably never wanted to know – existed. Post-rational critiques of his commercially successful, creatively questionable movies (he knew his addicted audience would transfer to celluloid, even if his talents didn't), and commentary on his recurring nightmare that his loyal fans had deserted him. They didn't. Seemingly, they never will. For, metaphorically, Elvis lives – and not just in 'Jailhouse Rock' ringtones, reissued albums and countless celebratory websites. Technology and marketing keep his story alive, and the fans love it.

In books, Agatha Christie, the best-selling author of the 1900s, wrote murder, she said, for her own enjoyment. But very many others enjoyed her narrative too. She produced popular stories by the bucketload, some as novels, others as plays. And then she encouraged their adaptation across media. *The Mousetrap* has run in London's West End for half a century, and new movie, radio and TV adaptations are sure-fire audience pullers. Through great storytelling, Dame Agatha captured the public's imagination.

Try this old chestnut and name a famous Belgian (those of Belgian extraction are exempt from this exercise). If Hercule Poirot wasn't on the list, then name four more. It just can't be done. That's not a sad reflection of an entire population of northern Europeans – rather, a flattering comment on the success of an enduring story, one that has transferred successfully across media. When audiences know a character so well that it defines an entire nation, then that's sticky.

Dame Agatha: started something sticky
Source: Historical Archive

The best old-media stories adapt and grow, building on their strengths, leaving new technologies to tell new or different parts of the story.

With more than two billion copies in book sales worldwide, translated into more than 100 languages, Christie beats Shakespeare in the fiction sales league. Yet for a pioneer in cross-media content production, she was a technological refusenik – preferring books to broadcasting, and refusing to buy a television for her home (although she did nip round to friends for an illicit fix when there was something on she fancied).

Today, Christie's plays are interactive – on the Agatha Christie website. Free and easy to use, this clearly written transfer of old content, freshly told, is not just for thriller aficionados. It's for anyone who wants to enjoy a great detective drama, a great story. Now audiences can partake, not just passively watch narrative as it unfolds, moving beyond the simple, guess-who-did-it participation of the books, films and serializations. It's a community with murder in mind.

Want to join in a discussion about Agatha, or any other detective writer? Try mysterynet.com, where you can solve it, get a clue, collect memorabilia, and get some tips on writing your own.

And if you're really a committed fan, then try the Agatha Christie Society site and join the club. 'Fun and fellowship for Dame Agatha's fans.' Sign up online, join in discussions, discover what events are being laid on, and receive the quarterly magazine, the *Christie Chronicle*, in print. Old media through new. The best old-media stories adapt and grow, building on their strengths, leaving new technologies to tell new or different parts of the story.

AGATHA CHRISTIE FACT BOX

- Sixteen plays, including *The Mousetrap*, which celebrated its fiftieth anniversary of an unbroken run in London's West End in 2002.
- Two billion books sold.
- More than 80 titles.
- Translated into 45 languages.
- Official website – agathachristie.com.
- The club – the Agatha Christie Society.
- The magazine – the *Christie Chronicle*.
- Number of films.
- First published 1920.

And this is what this book is about. Finding stories that transfer through time and across media. They don't have to go on forever, although it's nice if they do. Stories that pause for a while and come back in later years do good business too, because audiences enjoy a bit of nostalgia. We're searching for creative content that finds an audience, is told in many places, and makes a profit for its producers. And we'll look at the relationship between the truly original and the more common reliance on formulas – after all, there's a lot to be learned from that which has gone before.

So turn the page and let us tell you a story. Of how content of old becomes content of new – when it is powerful enough to carry itself through the ages and through any new media that come along the way. This is the story of sticky, addictive content. Of matching the message to the medium. Through stories from film, music, news and television, we'll discover common characteristics, how to attract a bigger audience, and how to remain true to one's art.

And, although it doesn't kill or irrevocably damage health, consumers do become addicted to big stories that are told well, particularly when they seem to be everywhere you turn. Like some rather powerful chemicals, the media is awash with sticky stories. Perhaps you wouldn't normally indulge. But temptation is in front of your eyes, and the medium has you in its grip. This is the story of addictive content.

THE STORYTELLERS

2

'An artist does not understand anything until he can do it.'

Leonardo da Vinci

Storytelling is a crucial but underexploited business tool. It's not too difficult to appreciate why.

Stories, surely, are for children. No self-respecting business person would reduce their complex business to a story. Business is real, about operations and strategy, profit and loss, customers and shareholders. Stories, by contrast, are fiction – the creation of the imagination, not of the real world. The only logic is in their structure; a beginning, middle and end. All the rest is fantasy.

In a world where the customer, not content, is king, and where the market determines success, isn't the producer's art diminished trying to second-guess which stories will gain the biggest audience? The best stories, one would expect, come from an individual's imagination, from someone who doesn't pander to market research. But now audiences are demanding to play a part; to pick the bits they like, when they like. To be treated as individuals. An audience of one.

So creative content is going interactive – and there's a lot of it about. We're spoiled for choice, and sometimes resentful of it. With simply so much content available, it's so much harder for anyone to find the good stuff – and even then it's easy to follow one's own path through the narrative – if a narrative exists at all. With readers taking control, storytellers, like the king's jester of old, must beware. In every new world, storytellers must learn what is acceptable to the audience, and what may lead to death.

ENDURING STORIES

The nineteenth-century novel was a weighty tome. The Brontës had plenty of time to craft their stories, deepen their characters, explore subtexts, develop themes. And readers, without the distractions of television, cinema or the Internet, could concentrate their free time on the leisurely pursuit of reading (after they had worked 16 hours, handwashed their clothes, put 14 children to bed, and fed the animals).

Few novels today build as slowly as nineteenth-century classics and hope to sell. These stories, with enduring themes of unrequited love and mismatched marriages, remain in demand today. But largely in other forms: as movies or television adaptations, and sometimes as educational software to help students prepare for examinations. Ang Lee's *Sense and Sensibility* (OK, he only directed it – the novel was written over the three years to 1798 by Jane Austen) could credibly be described as a Hollywood blockbuster, achieving a 1995 Oscar nomination for best picture and winning the award for best adapted screenplay. It grossed $142 million, which isn't bad for a 200-year-old story. Being dead and out of copyright, Jane Austen may not have made money out of the retelling of her story of British manners, but she would surely have been proud to be providing enjoyment almost 200 years after her death.

Did she write with the audience in mind? Possibly. But we can be sure it was for an audience with lots of time for reading, fewer choices of entertainment, and certainly not for the cinema. Austen continues to succeed in adaptations for the big screen and small, in videos and in education – she pops up regularly in English literature examinations. Jane Austen was – and is – a sticky storyteller. She transfers across media, and down through the ages. And she does so because, quite simply, she knew how to tell a great story. Addictive content doesn't have to be new. Audiences love the things they know.

Today, many novels read like movie scripts. Try a John Grisham. Fast-moving, snappy dialogue, a great story that's easily adaptable. That's not denigrating either genre. Films can transfer to novels; novels can transfer to films. Stories that can be retold in many media, for many years, are the ones that endure most profitably. But they can bomb if the right part of the story is not told in the right medium. Moving content from book to screen, or game to film, or from CD to concert hall, without thought for the characteristics of the medium and its appropriateness for the message, is just plain daft. Storytellers capture an audience when they understand their environment.

THE FORM OF STORY

Though we now think of stories as having a structure – the beginning, middle and end – there are plenty of examples where that's just not the case. But for most people, with strong expectations of form, anything less tends to be a disappointment. Artists may berate ungrateful audiences for their ignorance of new forms, but customers have the final say. Unusual structures generate smaller audiences – people just don't have the patience to work out a path and find their way around. And when audiences are small, revenues are small. Not sticking to established form, or at least adapting slowly, is for those who wish to communicate with an intimate audience.

Everyone understands the form of story because we are introduced to it so early in life. Fairy tales are usually the earliest stories, with the possible exception of nursery rhymes, that infants get to know. These are the traditional tales of good and evil that help our understanding of the world. For children, they also define what a story looks and sounds like – a hero, a villain or event, and a sequence leading to a climactic experience, usually good for the hero (unless he's done something bad, for which there is a payoff too). The Nordic languages use the word 'saga' for these kind of stories, avoiding the word 'fairies' – they rarely put in an appearance anyway.

These tales, with an emphasis on fantasy, are sometimes based loosely on historical events, usually told in the present tense, and have strong elements of drama and anticipation. Familiar they may be, but the audience's recurring question is 'What happens next?' Interactive games and science-fiction writers owe a debt of gratitude to the Brothers Grimm, who in turn cribbed the stories off cave walls and added a touch of imagination. These universal stories, whatever the culture from which they originate, attempt to explain the principles of life through narrative. Now, through interaction, explanation is only part of the story. Immersion is the added element.

Oh yes it is!

Let's explore fairy tales for a moment as one example of content that transfers across media – in this case, from the simple retelling of a book into theatrical production.

Most fairy tales were handed down through generations of retelling around the campfire or in the nursery. The most famous are traditional tales; others are newer collections by famous storytellers such as Hans Christian Anderson. These are the books that sell millions as each new generation of children is born. And they sell as picture books, videos films, sticker books, plastic toys and trips to Disneyland. Walt Disney was a great original storyteller who understood business. He knew Snow White would sell on film.

These sagas, fantasy tales, have loose structures around a central message. Flexible structures are great for retelling, embellishing, providing space for interaction, adapting for different environments, whether in the same medium or in new forms. With more than 200 versions of Cinderella and dozens of Jack and the Beanstalks, no two interpretations are exactly the same. Anything can happen along the path through a story, though there are certain links that remain common each time the story is told. And if it's not recited precisely word for word each time, who – above the age of three – actually cares? We all know the final outcome – the event from which there is no turning back. When Cinderella marries her prince, she can never go back to sitting in the cinders. It's the end of the story. Even interactive Internet games have an objective that, once set and then achieved, forms the culmination of the narrative. Nothing goes on forever.

A cave imprisoning a genie, a dark and frightening forest, a giant's castle, a boy who must overcome hurdles to please his father or save his head – this is the stuff of imagination. That of the writer, the producer, and ultimately the audience. These are the themes that endure, even if the interpretation is different between stories, or however those stories are told.

The most popular stories change with time. Pantomime, the British theatrical institution that takes fairy tales to the stage each Christmas, may appear to rely on the same old stories. The pace of change is slow and almost imperceptible. Harlequin Tom the Piper's Son and Goody Two Shoes, which were common Victorian stories, are largely unknown today. A century ago, when they were popular books, they were equally famous as pantomimes. They transferred, attracting audiences across generations and across social divides. They were sticky, from the day they were told in the nursery until the time they appeared on stage performed by the stars of the day.

Today, Cinderella, Aladdin and Dick Whittington are the most popular pantomimes, while Snow White continues to keep dwarfs in seasonal employment. They contain bags of contemporary references and twenty-first-century commentary to make them relevant to adults in the audience, with scripts changing, sometimes daily, to incorporate current affairs. And, insofar as a bit of community singing and the occasional call of 'He's behind you!' goes, pantomime is interactive.

Stories work subconsciously, educating and socializing, as well as entertaining. Success is dependent on understanding the politics, environment and society of the time of their creation – and using the right medium for the message – and finding themes and characters with which audiences will empathize. Renowned storytellers speak of connecting with the audience at an emotional level. Sociologist JSR Goodlad (1971) comments:

> When people watch drama, it is unlikely that they are indulging in the same sort of escape as they do when they sleep, take drugs, or drink alcohol. The likelihood is that they are not escaping *from* their social obligations, but escaping *into* an understanding of society, which is necessary for their participation in society.

Participation is more likely to be through consuming content than creating it, or even contributing to existing content. Not everyone has the ability to produce great material, even if they want to, and even if the tools of participation are commonplace. Just about everyone can write *something*, i.e. put words together in some order of semblance and get a basic message across. Some people can even launch a website and get their story to the wider world. But not many people are able to do it well enough to cause anyone else to want to spend time with their content. Storytelling is an art form, and the audience outnumbers performers.

In the 4000 years since the first written story was etched on to a wall, stories have been a metaphor for life. Everyone enjoys a good story. And the very best stories, told by great storytellers – not just people who thought they would knock something together because access is cheap these days – create communities. Content providers want to create communities too. A community of customers who come back.

Interactive content isn't new

If you thought interactivity was the grim reaper looking to put linear narrative to the sword (or scythe), history shows it is actually nothing new. Only the technologies are different. Themes survive the centuries so that even apparently original ideas probably aren't – they are just another interpretation of a hero's journey. Medieval literature was as non-linear, in its own way, as the new content of today. Often located in a green wood, a brave knight earns his spurs by appearing at the various events that happen there. He leaves a bigger and better person. The story is about space and what happens in it as much as it is about character and events. Richard Fell, at the BBC's Fictionlab, which develops drama for interactive television, broadband and the Web, says:

> The shape of the medieval story is the equivalent of what we can do today with non-linear narrative. Today, you can actually immerse yourself into the story in different ways in its own kind of story space. It is less prescriptive, more interpretive, more specific to the medium or culture and owned, to a greater or lesser degree, by the audience themselves.

Just as it was in Greek amphitheatres. There is no ancient Greek word for 'theatre', only for the action of participating in theatre. Even today, when done well, theatre is not a passive experience. It is a story with which the audience becomes emotionally involved, participating in the lives of characters placed before them.

Interactive stories, and the non-interactive form, can happily co-exist and build audiences for one another. Content transfer when audiences feel involved.

But will audience want to interact with stories more fully rather than just watching or listening? Doesn't interaction verge on playing a game, and isn't gaming a young person's thing? With real-life stories, how many people have given up their newspapers to get their daily news from the Web and plot their own way through to discover more? Very few – so far. But there's little to fear and a lot to learn from history. Interactive stories, and the non-interactive form, can happily co-exist and build audiences for one another. It's interactive horses for interactive courses. Content transfers when audiences feel involved.

Participation has been around for as long as content. Elizabethan theatre wasn't a place where one politely kept quiet for a three-hour passage of the play. Heckling was as prevalent at the Globe as it is at a modern-day hustings. Newspapers print opinion, and outraged readers send letters to the editor. When Opportunity Knocked on UK television in the 1960s, the studio clapometer, a primitive example of interactive technology, measured the audience's preference for a singer, comedian or magician. But it was the audience's postal vote that counted. It's all interaction. It happens when the audience is immersed in the story.

Today, technology allows storytellers to offer audiences more sophisticated ways of participating, allowing them to affect narrative. Whether the magician or contortionist wins the talent show and returns the following week influences subsequent content. Contestants who are voted out of game shows may be the ones on whom future ratings – or publicity – depend. Like medieval dramas, which had strong underlying structure, audiences can influence the path, but they are not in overall control. Content is created before paths can be navigated. It must continue to work, for example, even if the audience's decisions lead to weaker characters surviving. There is always another event, character or prop that can help the narrative along.

Of course, the audience can be allowed to interact with content without affecting its delivery. So websites and radio and TV programmes contain competitions that are just for fun. Letters pages of newspapers, widely read, are just about the only section of the publication in which the customers can participate. But this kind of interaction, effectively providing free content to the publisher, doesn't influence the flow of narrative. That is decided by producers. It is 'professional' content, untainted by less well-crafted material from outsiders. The audience is never really in control.

CONVENTIONS BUILD COMMUNITIES –THAT DON'T INTERACT ...

Some argue that it's not the idea of drama or storytelling for audiences to participate. The point is to be led somewhere by someone else, to be a passive participant in a sea of discovery. We marvel at the imaginations of others, agree to unwritten rules about the environment in which the story is told – such as sitting in the dark of an auditorium, quiet save for the unwrapping of sweets – and allow ourselves to be immersed in the content.

These rules are important, yet they are unspoken. Digital media are said to break established rules, putting audiences in control. But both old media and new create communities when common conventions are shared. New media create new communities, with different rules, but there are rules nonetheless. Send an email in capital letters, the equivalent of shouting, and it stands out as rude. Fail to learn the code of text messaging, and, in the event you manage to access your messages, you're unlikely to understand much of what is being said.

The conventions of old media are so familiar that consumers are usually blind to them. The front page of the newspaper contains the most important news and is designed to be read first (unless you're into sport, in which case you read from the back). In music, singles are the best tracks from the album, and you only buy them if you're a teenager or a granny. These are the expectations in the old-media environment.

With rules, customers understand what is expected of them. They may be unspoken, and they may adapt slowly over time, but communities are built on rules. And you have to be very, very skilled – or lucky – to break them and bring the audience along with you.

Dungeons and Dragons, the seminal science-fiction games books of the 1980s, was a precursor to electronic games. The form was a book, but the story wasn't a novel. The content broke the conventions of the environment, yet it still guided the audience through the story. The reader, an active participant, follows a path of their own determination, taking forks on decision trees, battling evil, collecting trophies, rarely following the same path twice. The addictive content spawned an entire genre and afflicted a generation of young gamers well into their middle years. It transferred across media, into PC games and character models, and continues to have a committed following.

Conversely, linear storytelling shows little sign of being consumed by the rise of interactivity. It has strengths all of its own, which audiences appreciate. We like it. We're used to it. We're educated in it. And familiarity with linear stories is passed through the generations. Despite the ease with which children take to digital technologies, they are socialized in the conventions of stories – across a multitude of media – almost from birth.

Just as audiences understand, and are fond of, old conventions in which they are not expected to participate, they also have an attachment to old media. Analogue and print forms will be around for a long time to come. Large numbers of people either don't want to go digital or can't afford to do so. Many millions of state pensioners, for example, can't afford new media, never mind understand it. Up to one-quarter of UK households don't expect to be online – ever. If people want to sell these people new content, then they are going to have to produce it in ways that can be received.

And because audiences actually like old media, their early demise is unlikely. Just as television didn't kill radio, the Internet won't replace other kinds of content, although patterns of usage may change (radio, incidentally, is listened to more than television is viewed in the UK, proving there's life in 100-year-old technologies yet). The danger for old media is a general erosion of the share of the audience's time, not a dramatic one. The UK's national newspaper market, for example, has suffered a slow rate of decline for more than a decade, beginning before the widespread adoption of the Internet. Audiences have not made a mass switch to interactive replacements. But younger people are slow to take up old habits. While old-media audiences are declining very, very slowly, the drop is steepest among the young. They watch less television (but always have), read fewer newspapers (but always have), and buy fewer books (but always have). They do, however, listen to most music, they are heavyweight movie buffs, and they spend lots of time online. In short, stories that transfer across media are of interest to young people too – if one can find the addictive content.

One of the largest hurdles for interactive storytelling is not about audience expectations or demand, but is central to production. In a nutshell, it's hard to do. New forms of storytelling are just so difficult for producers to get right. An unknown quantity, producers not only have to think up ideas for content that can work in their preferred medium and address the practicalities in getting it produced, they then have to create demand where at present there is little.

Even in games, the most advanced of the interactive media, producing any kind of new content is extraordinarily time consuming. Large teams, working for lengthy periods, mean very high costs. One can expect to spend at least two years from the concept of an idea until it sees the light of day as a piece of software. Narrative interactive games require more than just the characterization, plot and themes that are central to stories in linear media. Gamers expect great graphics, the thrill of a chase, a competitive edge. To date, no one has written an interactive game that is wonderful both as a game and a significant piece of new literature.

Transferring content from games to film has worked occasionally, as it has with magazines. But games are still more dependent on visual imagery than story, and are likely to remain confined by the medium.

... AND COMMUNITIES THAT DO INTERACT

Although old media are enduring, they have to adapt the way they tell their stories if they are to remain relevant. Hundreds of years of refining stories to fit into the media formats we know have just gone up in smoke. Novels that were crafted beautifully in several hundred pages now have to be slimmer. Journalists who know what a story looks like now have to write it even more crisply – possibly for more than one outlet. New media flows in new ways, and storytellers must help audiences navigate the rapids. Sometimes it's called 'dumbing down' – appealing to the lowest possible denominator. But it's not – providing one produces content while understanding that audiences select content from many sources. People come back to those places that provide the right content, in the right context, for their purpose. Sometimes they want lengthy narrative; at other times they want short summaries. Sometimes they want to be guided; other times they want to find their own way.

Each new medium arrives with its own characteristics, some of which are suitable for different bits of the story, and some that won't work for certain parts at all. Clever content producers use digital media to extend their story, but don't expect one size to fit all. But elements that make compelling content have common characteristics, the conventions that audiences understand. In news, for example, all stories tell the audience something new with genuine surprises, and have tensions between characters (there are good guys and bad guys in most news stories) and a degree of familiarity. At least some of these elements need to appear in whichever medium the content appears if it is to follow the conventions that the audience understands.

Traditional storytelling, of the hero and villain type, hasn't crumbled away as content has become more prevalent. It provides the context by which audiences identify characters and themes – even for factual content. The fundamental questions posed in drama are present in news reporting. Editors follow form and structure in making news – audiences can choose to follow it in narrative form, or interact to discover more about background, facts, or related stories.

THE QUESTIONS

Does the story have conflict?
Who are the main players?
Who are the good guys and who are the villains?
What events are forcing the main characters to change and adapt?
What life-changing decisions have to be made along the way?
Who are the mentors – independent third parties – who can influence the main players?
What is the climactic event that this story is, or could be, moving towards?
What happens next?
Who cares?

Interactive storytelling works because it doesn't threaten the established ways of telling stories – providing existing media adapt and tell the right bits of the story for their format – giving up those parts that others do better and filling the gap with even better content. Existing storytellers with loyal audiences can extend into new channels and have the best of both worlds – or fail in both. For example, if news is delivered faster on the Internet than it is in newspapers, than the press should tell shorter stories faster on the Web, using its interactive potential to move audiences through a story's history and background, allowing sections of the audience to communicate with one another about topics of interest, even to disagree with the publisher's editorial line.

Done correctly, when new media lessons are learned, audiences delight in new ways of interacting with content. It may not be one to one, but it can often seem so. The best interactive creative content works for audiences, works for storytellers, and works for creative people who want to share their ideas in as many ways as possible.

Today, a single story can express itself one way on the Web, in another way in print, and in another way in the cinema. No one has to see them all to enjoy or understand the narrative, and sometimes seeing more than one part leads to disappointment in the others. People who enjoyed *Hitchhiker's Guide to the Galaxy* in print are sometimes unimpressed with its adaptation on television. Those who heard it first on radio feel a sense of ownership – they discovered it first, and they know all the lines in audio, video and print. That pictures are better on radio is a popular refrain of, as one might expect, radio producers. Nevertheless, each medium brings a new audience for the *Hitchhiker's Guide*, and although not much of the story in each medium was new, cross-promotion of the material resulted in transferable, loyal audiences. And not inconsiderable profit.

THE NEW PRODUCTION VOCABULARY

It may have worked profitably for Douglas Adams, but taking old forms and sticking it across new media isn't a guaranteed path to success. The temptation to reproduce existing content in every possible medium is natural, because it's easy and relatively cheap. The practice is far from new. BBC radio news in the 1920s was presented by dinner-jacketed announcers reading from newspapers. It was informative – and very dull. But because listeners didn't have any expectations of this new medium, and producers were also finding their feet, it must at least have felt appropriate. Rather like touching one's cap to a blind man, it was the done thing.

Producers create new content from a reference point of old content: they know what works, what attracts an audience. Producing interactive content involves an entire new vocabulary for producers from the established media. But it's easier in some genres than others. Most people recognize the format of games and quizzes. They are usually spread over a short timeframe with a small variety in the challenges along the way, and often with an increasing level of difficulty as the game progresses. Even Monopoly gets harder as the hotels go up.

That's the case whether it's a board game, a party game, a television quiz, or electronic software with multiple players on the Internet. Ask a nine-year-old to explain how to play a game, and you'll be told, 'Not now, I'm nearly on level four.' Games are challenges, whatever the medium, and understanding that people have to beat the competition – even if it's their own earlier score – makes them addictive.

Humans are the only species to create challenges as games, purely for fun. Because this trait appears to originate in our genetic make-up, whatever format comes along, games will remain a central piece of addictive content. Newspapers have crosswords, magazines have quizzes, television has its game shows, and sport – games in themselves – heightens its excitement with betting.

Other animals may enjoy play, but no other species actually creates structured, challenging games as an end in themselves. Set an interactive course for a mouse and reward it with a lump of cheese and it will complete the challenge and take the prize. But give a gang of mice a slab of cheddar and expect them to create an obstacle course in which winner takes all, and it's simply not going to work (but there's an idea for a computer game, surely).

Producers do not know quite how to handle new media, fumbling around with the best intentions, experimenting until it looks like it might work. Once any medium takes off, there's a rush to produce more of the stuff. Almost all books, records, films, videos and TV programmes produced each year are not very good. Now websites, email messages, downloadable music and video files are fighting for audience attention.

A fear that having too much available inevitably results in poorer content is longstanding. When there are few sources of content generating relatively high levels of audience (and hence income), it could be argued that, proportionally, the quality of material is naturally higher. There are more resources available to pay for less content.

Now anyone can produce content. The result: there may be much more low-quality content knocking around, but at least it's cheap, low-quality content, and sometimes even homemade, low-quality content. But that doesn't necessarily mean the good stuff has been wiped off the face of the planet. Quality is in the eye of the beholder. Some audiences like art-house movies, others prefer Hollywood blockbusters. New technologies –

in this case, cheaper digital cameras, for example – don't wipe out either. They do mean more people can enter the film business, but they won't all compete with existing forms of delivery. There's room for both – and an awful lot more.

In the early days of radio broadcasting in the UK, the BBC believed its duty was to prevent audiences getting hooked, possibly causing psychological damage to its listeners in the process.

'The listener must recognise that a definite obligation rests on him to choose intelligently from the programmes offered to him,' warned the Corporation's annual handbook in 1930, and because many in the audience couldn't be trusted to know what was best for them, it encouraged listeners to switch off by inserting five-minute breaks between programmes.

Most mass-media organizations don't face this issue today, suffering the plight of audiences switching off of their own accord. The old joke is that many people tune in to watch the adverts because they are the most interesting thing on the box.

There may be some truth in it. Advertising has to be sticky: not to itself, but to its product, otherwise the producers – the advertising agencies – lose the business. In units of about 30 seconds, advertisers are storytellers. And like the king's jester, they create something which, in its best form, can be told over and over again, to an audience that never tires of the subject.

ADVERTISERS ARE STORYTELLERS

Advertising doesn't exclusively use storytelling to sell its wares, but like the fairy tale, a great advertising campaign is enduring and gets retold, with scope for embellishment each time, and can transfer across many media. More than one-fifth of adults claim to enjoy television commercials as much as the programmes they surround (the *Guardian*, 2001), and a similar number say the advertisements give them something to talk about.

Like a story, it may have interwoven themes, regular characters, and a single overarching message that the author wishes to communicate. Unlike stories, though, which are often told for their own sake, advertising advocates a commercial sales message.

Some of the most enduring campaigns, those that have run for many years, present new twists to stories that began decades ago, well outside the living memory of the brand managers and advertising agency staff telling the story today. Heineken, a beer, refreshed the parts others couldn't reach in the 1970s and 1980s. In the 1990s and today, it is still 'refreshing', with 30-second sketches that explain just how. Same story, with a twist. Like the many ways of retelling Jack and the Beanstalk. When the Oxo family finally retired after 30 years, it became a story in itself. Three years later, and with new advertising that hadn't quite struck its old chord, Oxo put together another family story, and started another chapter. Bearded Captain Birdseye, a fish-finger selling old seadog, was pensioned off after many years' service peddling processed meals, eventually to be reinstated as a clean-shaven, hunky young man in a sailor suit. A story which works may need refreshing to rediscover its relevance to a new generation of mothers for whom muscles are more attractive than facial hair. But if the story works, it is rarely worth ditching. And if freshening it up doesn't work (which it didn't for Birdseye, so a whiskery captain was re-employed) – one can always revert to tested traditional tales.

Advertisers face the same dilemmas as anyone else who wants to get an audience to hear their tale. In the interactive world, having a good story or idea is only part of the battle. Getting people to hear it, understand it, act upon it and then come back is the harder part. If the audience shuns the media, but one feels they would still be open to the story, then the challenge is about how to reach them. Advertising agency boss Greg Delaney explains:

> We don't have any prejudice in favour of stories, or humour, or warmth or human involvement. We will use what works to advocate a point of view in order to attract attention. But it's easier to tell stories in 30 seconds than it is in longer periods. Research groups show time and again that people like a beginning, middle and end. People look for meaning. So we make those 30 seconds work really hard, using every single film and editing technique to speed up the process and take people through the story.

Advertisers seek share of mind; perhaps not quite as much as share of purse, but it's a very good start along the way to a profitable relationship. The stories within advertisements can lead to products of themselves and new sales ideas that embody the brand. UK toilet tissue Andrex tells its story of softness with Labrador puppies (a dozen or so on the set at each shoot, as they get exhausted filming each part of a scene; dogs, notoriously, also can't act). In Britain, Labradors are almost synonymous with toilet paper (although Guide Dogs for the Blind could also stake a reasonable claim to the breed). See the dog – the character – and the story is half told.

Advertising for Yellow Pages, in which fictional character JR Hartley trudged round bookshops trying to find a copy of his own *Fly Fishing*, led to such demand for the book, which of course didn't exist, that someone had to write it. The advertisement transferred to the book, which sold the phone directory. Advertising helps make content sticky.

COMMERCIAL BREAKDOWN

Advertisers today face the trauma of large numbers of passive consumers splitting into thousands of splinter groups, demanding more from their stories. If advertising has been told in 30-second bursts, or as classifieds in the columns of newspapers, then there's no certainty it will remain that way. For media owners, classified advertising revenues, which flow with the economic cycle, are often first under pressure as employers impose recruitment freezes, affecting job ads. Then people hold off moving house, affecting property ads, and buy fewer investments, affecting financial ads. Interactive, personalized media weaken the clustering of classifieds into established mass channels. Instead, buyers can find classified information more appropriate to their individual circumstances faster and more accurately on the Internet. Job ads migrate to Monster.com and financial products to other online aggregators, taking commissions away from intermediaries and advertising from traditional media. A slump in advertising revenues equates to a slump in cash for content production, leading to fewer reasons for audiences to return to established media. Only addicted audiences need to come back.

In the UK, television commercials have traditionally been produced in units of 30 seconds and flung together in batches, lasting about three minutes – the advertising equivalent of a collection of short stories brought together in a slim volume. To save confusion with the real story for which viewers have turned on, television commercial breaks have health warnings – a slide announcing 'End of Part One' or the title of the show, forewarning audiences to brace themselves for a barrage of sales-people masquerading as storytellers. Viewers who get up to make coffee or grab a beer, zap to another channel, or fast-forward through the break if they're watching something recorded earlier are inadvertently cutting the production budgets of the content they enjoy (except for a vocal minority who swear that the ads are better than the programmes). According to Forrester Research (2001), six out of ten viewers no longer pay attention to prime-time commercials, and ethnographic research from the London Business School suggests that watching advertisements is a minority sport that often takes part in small groups, and even then only so that friends and family can disparage the products.

Soon, audiences won't even have to make the decision about whether to skip ads – technology can do that for them. With personal video recorders, ad breaks can be jumped, programmes paused, masses of content stored on hard disk. Advertisers won't keep paying for adverts people don't watch, and both viewers and advertisers will have so much more media choice.

The USA has never been apologetic about advertisements interrupting programmes, where one second the audience can be following a drama serial, and the next being sold laxatives or health insurance. Then back again to the gripping drama before the beer is even out of the fridge. Pressing the remote control to zap ads can be more effort than it's worth, but trying at least gives couch potatoes some small measure of exercise. In the US, the network television audience has already been decimated, first by cable and then by satellite viewing. The main channels that used to receive almost a 90% share in the 1980s today achieve about 65%. Bigger, better, more compulsive content is in even greater demand to keep shares up, or lure audiences elsewhere. The best storytellers can name their price.

If they are to keep audiences hooked to content, television commercial breaks will become shorter. Increasingly, commercial messages will be integrated within content. That might not appear to be the trend right now, where to make up for lower costs per advertisement (because of smaller audiences), channels are pumping out *more* commercial airtime – the very thing audiences turn away from. This doesn't sound a logical plan for building customer loyalty. In 2000, British TV regulators allowed commercial television additional airtime for ad breaks in peak time, enabling stations under financial pressures to run longer and more frequent breaks. Earlier, they had relaxed rules on masthead broadcasting – television programmes based on magazine titles, affording another opportunity to raise revenues for content (and profit). But many in the audience turn away by habit – many zappers of advertising breaks instinctively know when to turn back to continue watching programmes, not ads (Ritson, 2002). So new ways of paying for content just have to come.

Product placement, endemic in movies, widespread on US television, is creeping into Europe. We've come full circle from the early days of radio, the origins of soap opera, when Lux, the toilet soap manufacturer, put its name to almost 1,000 episodes of audio drama over a period of 20 years. *Adam and Eva*, a 1935 production, found the emotional – and practical – truth to capturing young sweet love:

Jane: Poor Amy! Everybody noticed she wasn't having a good time! It's a shame. After all, Amy is quite pretty …

Sue: And the men like her, really. Why, my brother says he'd go for Amy in a big way if it weren't for her complexion …

Jane: No, really, did he? Gee – let's help Amy! Let's send her some Lux Toilet Soap—

Sue: And I'll put in a note about how it guards against 'cosmetic skin'. That's all the hint she needs …

Today, that's a commercial. Product placement. Something beyond sponsorship. We'd be moving wholly back to it if the audience wasn't so advertising-savvy, more resentful of stories being used overtly for selling when the pretence is entertainment. Audiences don't mind advertising, particularly when it entertains, and especially when it offsets the costs of content. But people can't be duped, and too much other quality material is competing for their time without intrusion from commercial messages. (If you do fancy a fix of Lux radio drama, some episodes are available at oldetimeradio.com, most are on CD, and a handful of American radio stations still play repeats.)

Not all content has the magical spice that makes it addictive. Producing great creative content is a collaborative art, which begins with a compelling idea. But so much can go wrong along the way in the attempt to develop it into a successful business. Sure-fire hits are myths. Nobody has a guaranteed formula for producing addictive, quality content that finds an audience every time. Indeed, many producers abhor any search for a formula, believing it to be detrimental to true originality.

Easier to find are the essential forms to which creative content must comply. Form is the artistically correct term for consistent, strong structure around which content is built. And if one can tell a story along the way, then the audience is much more likely to follow one through a path. That means having something great to say and communicating it effectively. It means choosing the right medium for the message. Selecting a strong storyteller – perhaps an intermediary such as a newscaster or star talent – or speaking with an independent voice or a personal one. Making brilliant use of craft skills – design, music, navigation, page design and illustrations for the Web; or performance, script and cinematography for video or film; or words, pictures and headlines in news. Finally, it means encouraging the audience to switch between media to move with the story in all its forms.

Production depends on many people, even if the idea originated with an individual genius whose sole talent is to craft great stories. A neat idea may be fine as a concept, but the torture of getting it produced, whatever the medium, is a complex process that demands the creativity, motivation and discipline of others. Content produced in isolation can result in introspective, indulgent work. It requires collaboration between storytellers, business managers and craftspeople. In the digital world, the audience is a collaborator too.

Although everything starts with a good idea, great content relies on tenacity, teamwork and talent. Money helps, as does a commitment from everyone along the line in the process. And sometimes that's just so difficult to achieve. Creative businesses, by definition, are full of creative people. And creative people are professional people, committed to their art and usually more than committed to playing their part in creating brilliant work. They are often far from easy to manage, with great work resulting from a combination of commitment and talent rather than good planning. But good planning there must be. Creation comes more easily when there is a plan to follow.

Ideas don't come from nowhere. Hollywood studios, for example, have story departments – entire teams whose job it is to develop characters, themes, tensions, dramas. And more often than not, to decide to throw them out at some stage because they just don't work. But once something starts to come together, and the story moves into production, it enters a well-established process of manufacturing, testing (audience research) and retuning. It is a process that combines planning with creative instinct.

Final creative decisions rest with the leader. This is the role of the director or editor. The author of the production. The 'sir' figure who carries the can when audiences fail to flock.

If the director is the CEO, then his boss is a producer (the chairperson) who has overall responsibility for key hires and turning a profit, and who works with a team of creative professionals (the board of directors), each of whom manages their own divisions of craftspeople. People follow great directors. They command enormous respect and associated enormous pay packets, like their CEO counterparts, because producing material that substantial numbers of people want to buy isn't easy.

The challenge for content producers is for the attention of an audience. Directors may feel secure and be in great demand in their chosen medium. But content that exists only in a single medium is at risk in its isolation. At the beginning of the twenty-first century, the trend in newspaper sales is downwards. So are sales of CDs. So is television viewing. People still want news, music and drama, but they watch, listen and consume in new ways as well as traditional ones. Audiences mix and match their consumption habits. As they are presented with greater choice, they take it. Their spend – of time and money – across any single medium is diluted.

Content creators, while specializing in their chosen medium, should have an eye on the ability of their content to transfer. Although sensible, the concept that people should specialize in one medium, perfecting their art, need not always apply. Leonardo da Vinci was an engineer, a writer, a philosopher and an artist. Segmentation by discipline is a modern business constraint. And it is leading to a divide between old media and new.

Sometimes, old-media hands are slow to transfer or upgrade their skills (or downgrade, as some may see it) into new media. At the start of the Internet era, many established media businesses were scornful of the idea that technologies could erode their established market positions. People won't read newspapers on the Web, said some. Readers prefer something portable, flexible and cheap, and that doesn't break when someone spills coffee on it. People won't want to download music on to mobile devices because it simply takes too long and they don't know where to look. Habits change along with technologies. Before audiences find out where to look, and before downloads are fast, established businesses must change.

If one can build stories that transfer across media, that attract an audience that spreads the word and comes back, then one has found a business that can be profitable.

New-media people too often become overly involved in the technology of their medium, failing to take the trouble to understand the relationship of content to its audience. Audiences buy content, not technologies. Most people with access to new media consume it alongside their existing technologies. Radio *and* TV. MP3 *and* CDs. Internet *and* newspapers. Patterns of consumption may change, but rarely does one medium completely replace another. But whether one operates in new media or old – maybe even both – and whatever form of content one tells, if one can build stories that transfer across media, that attract an audience that spreads the word and comes back, then one has found a business that can be profitable. Now to make it sticky.

CHECKLIST: STORYTELLING

- Produce stories with flexible structures. These are best for retelling, embellishing and interacting with, and accordingly are easier to transfer across media.
- Find an enduring theme that adapts with the times.
- Create community around the story – communities keep people coming back.
- Collaborate for success. Individual talents combine to tell bigger stories.
- Familiarity doesn't exclude the possibility of surprise.
- Tell the audience something new.

REFERENCES

Forrester Research, 'Empowered customers, not mass audiences', Forrester. Com, December 2001.

J.S.R. Goodlad, *A Sociology of Popular Drama*, Heinemann, 1971.

The *Guardian*, 'The pulse: commercial breakdown', the *Guardian*, 28 August 2001.

Mark Ritson, 'Are you paying attention?', *Financial Times*, 14 May 2002.

MAKING HITS

3

'A film should have a beginning, middle and end. But not necessarily in that order.'

If all creative content were 100% sticky, then nothing new would ever be created. Reliable hit factories would churn out material, attract all available creative resource, and capture the entire audience. Audiences, knowing what they want, would never seek anything new.

Fortunately, audiences are more fickle. While many old stories are regularly rejuvenated, telling stories to create sticky content is a fashion business. Around core characteristics and themes and a structure that is known to work, new content is created. Some content is created without the support of structure, and that's a riskier proposition that we'll explore further in Chapter 6. Most digital storytellers want to be successful, and success is more assured when one understand the constraints of structure and the characteristics of media.

New Digital media provide much more of what was previously a scarce resource – access to audiences. It's easier to get a story on air, a music track distributed, a book deal signed. Fashion changes, sometimes incrementally, sometimes dramatically, so new content is always in demand. At the same time, it's also true that a lot of content, like style, never goes out of fashion.

Fashionable content can have an enormous commercial and creative impact for a short period of time, transferring over many media, before falling into the creative graveyard. That's OK, it's the nature of fashion. The world is littered with films, books, websites, music that becomes a phenomenal hit, which everyone seems to be talking about. And then, as quickly as the story rose, it falls away and is rarely heard of again.

But successful, sticky fashion reinvents itself constantly. The business of fashion is enduring, even if individual products only have a very short lifespan. To stay at the pinnacle of fashion, artists must capture an essence that will be in eternal demand. Dying is a good way, as the estates of Elvis Presley and James Dean testify. Kurt Cobain could perhaps be said to have made suicide fashionable, and Nirvana are richer for it. Elvis's audience at first grew older with him. After his death, his story is constantly updated – even remixed by nightclub DJs.

Stickiness exists in degrees, a progression that moves from the mildly sticky – the kids' paper glue of content – to the ultimate, never-to-be-removed, fanatical loyalty – sticky content's superglue. The further one moves up this adhesive continuum, the easier it is to transfer content between media.

Star Wars, for example, generates such loyalty that the film, books and toys all benefit each other, the whole becoming more than the sum of its parts. We know where the core is – it's a film from 1977 that cost $11 million to make but eventually paid back half a billion at the box office. But the franchise extends across media, generating even more income, and the story lives forever. That's good news for its creator George Lucas, who waived his director's fee in return for merchandising rights. Subsequent merchandise and box-office income allowed Lucas to establish his production company Lucasfilm, building future episodes free from the usual interference from a Hollywood studio.

The sticky Star Wars story lives forever

Source: reuters.popperfoto

Today, starwars.com provides the authorized digital intergalactic experience, with opportunities to reminisce with one's favourite bit of the story, interact with other fans and, of course, buy Star Wars goodies. The antithesis comes in a glut of counter-Star Wars sites, where people who hate the Star Wars industry interact with like-minded souls. They do not have much impact on the profitability of the Star Wars franchise, but at least kindred spirits are brought together.

The development of communities around content extends the shelf-life of the story. The second most visited Star Wars website, www.theforce.net ('your daily dose of Star Wars' runs the addiction-accepting strapline), is run by a Baptist pastor in Michigan who was too young to see the original film when it first came out. It attracts more than 50,000 unique visitors a month, feeds fans' obsessions with Star Wars trivia and breaks Star Wars news that the official site may be withholding. The official site may have an audience ten times the size of theforce.com, but it doesn't come with the gossip and insider leaks that unofficial sites offer. It is the unauthorized biography to the sanctioned version – both have merits, both are true accounts, and both are sought eagerly by addicts.

At the other, old-economy end of the scale, *Star Wars Fact Files*, a print publication, began weekly serialization as a stand-alone magazine in 2001. Jedi followers on earth pay a few pounds each week to collect the definitive guide to everything Star Wars, ultimately buying an attractive binder to keep the collection safe. True addicts collect the merchandise, from pencils and erasers, to a vintage Boba Fett figurine with rocket-firing backpack (never released commercially), which trades for about £20,000.

The Star Wars enterprise has become so big that when a rumour that the British government would have to recognize Jedi as an official religion if enough people declared they were Jedi Knights on the 2001 census form, more than 10,000 people claimed allegiance. The idea, spread originally among die-hard fans by viral email, soon became a way to cock a snoop at the government. Today, Jedi is formally recognized as a religion in the UK.

HIGH STAKES, HIGH REWARDS, LOTS OF FAILURES

The risks are huge and the chances of success small, so there are only two reasons why anyone would want to make a living creating sticky content. One is that when it works, the payback potential is massive. This is a business for creative entrepreneurs who don't mind losing their shirts. The second is that many artists are not businesspeople; indeed, they are sometimes a little nuts or at the very least somewhat temperamental. Many create solely for the purpose of creation. Some very fine art comes from it.

But creation for oneself is hardly a viable business proposition for anyone but the most exceptional of talents. Better to find a methodological approach to creating sticky content, and then apply it across media to reach the maximum audience potential for its type.

'For its type' is an important clarification. If you want to maximize the audience, you must deliver those elements in which the greatest number of people will be interested, and deliver the package better than anyone else. And if your content isn't as good as others in the market, then play around with distribution or schedules. Don't fight fire with fire. Fight fire with water. The provision of a clear alternative is a stronger hand than a weak imitation of the market leader.

Some content creators want to make money more than content. Only fools and artists are actually happy to lose money. The wise seek to produce great content that delights audiences, is creatively fulfilling, and generates a reasonable return on investment.

Sometimes, playing it safe creatively provides a reliable source of income with which to experiment with other bits of content. Theatre proprietors could pack every seat in the house providing bingo in the afternoons and wrestling in the evenings. Both are addictive content with loyal followings, guaranteed to bring revenues. Bingo and wrestling could finance artier shows, the kind that wouldn't fill an auditorium in a hundred years. Lighter entertainment provides, in the phrase of Jeremy Isaacs, former chief executive of UK broadcaster Channel 4, the means to the end. Popular shows, attracting large audiences, which subsidize the riskier, lower-audience productions.

If you don't believe that something as old-fashioned as bingo or wrestling could be sticky in the modern day, then consider this: the organization formerly known as the WWF and now called World Wrestling Entertainment[1] (WWE) hosts live bouts every other day in a North American city, and annually attracts 2.5 million screaming youths baying for blood. These live events provide content for TV shows, webcasts and pay-per-view programming, with the high-profile TV shows generating demand for licensed merchandise, videos, books and magazines.

In transferring the brand online, the WWE has created a sticky property that its audience is willing to pay for. Although most of its main website is

---

[1] After a spat in the high court, the wrestling WWF abandoned its name in 2002 in order to prevent confusion between costumed grapplers and the pandas of the World Wildlife Fund.

open, pay-per-view webcasts and merchandise sales generate significant revenues. But with only four million unique monthly users, sizable though that is the online presence doesn't match its old-media print equivalent. WWE's magazines enjoy a subscriber base almost 50% higher.

Wrestling, which used to attract an audience of the elderly and somewhat downmarket, is now cool, aggressive and unapologetically aimed at youth. The story, a hit with 12–25-year-old males, may be pre-scripted and involve unlikely role models in strange make-up and spangled lycra, but it generates more pay-per-view revenues than any other sport in the world. Sixteen thousand tickets for one live event in 2001 sold out in 36 minutes, and 170,000 viewers bought passes to watch it on television at an average cost of £11 per pay-per-view ticket, bringing in revenues of around £5 million. This is hit, transferable content, which understands its audience and knows how to tell different parts of its story in different media. Some is free (on the Web or terrestrial television), some costs relatively modest sums (the magazine), and others are a little further up the price scale (event tickets and pay-per-view). The hard-earned money of the audience – or their parents – finds its way to the creators of hit content easily and in lavish amounts.

BEYOND SELF-ACTUALIZATION

Rewards can be huge, considering creative businesses produce hardly anything of practical value. They don't keep the wind and the rain out of the house, they don't feed the family, and they don't even provide a mod con, an entirely new way of washing the pets or steaming vegetables. Music, films, television and magazines are, on the whole, entirely redundant for any purpose other than forgetting about everything else. And even that escape function is under threat, as audiences crave greater participation.

Despite the apparent uselessness of much creative content, as economies become more affluent, consumers are increasingly happy to spend more of their wealth on diversionary activities such as entertainment. When you've gorged enough food, gained comfort from a sense of belonging, and achieved self-esteem, what else is there to do?

This is the new peak of Abraham Maslow's famous hierarchy of needs, with food at its base and self-actualization at the summit. Self-actualization is achieving a calling, making music, writing books, enjoying culture –

and with digital media, we can do so much more of it. He might not have known it when he wrote his theory in the 1960s, but Abe was foretelling that creative businesses, digitally delivered, would be the pinnacle of his pyramid within half a century. Now where does one go from the peak of a pyramid? You get even more self-actualized, or you dream bigger dreams.

Most people in the western world are in the fortunate position of having plenty to eat, drink and buy. We are cautioned to exercise restraint, to eat less, drink less, consume less.

Instead, once dishwashers, juicers, or whatever other indispensable new invention that makes life easier are commonplace in the home, consumers spend money on things that are in part mindless and in part emotionally stimulating – a conflict that is somehow reconciled in creative content. More disposable income than ever is being spent on entertainment, stories, games, even ringtones for mobile phones. If you make great creative content, then there's a market for it. But it's got to be good to get noticed.

THE CREATIVE MIX

The creation of content begins with an idea, but before it gets to market, a process swings into action, mixing craft skills and creative art to transform the original vision into the final product. It is a process fraught with intellectual traps and practical difficulties – tensions between talent and technicians – which, when it works, produces something powerful with a value way in excess of the sum of its raw parts and a bit over for profit. But getting new content to work to the satisfaction of an audience large enough to make a profit is beyond the wit of many. An idea is the easy bit. Development, launch and selling are much harder.

Simplifying the complexities of all human interaction, there are two types of employees in creative businesses of old – the creatives and the business-people. The businesspeople tolerated the creatives as being a necessary, if somewhat indisciplined bunch of layabouts, one or two of whom would be geniuses and some of whom would lay golden eggs. The creatives believed that the businesspeople were bastards out to steal the eggs, tolerating them only in return for a salary, an expense account, and space and time to lay.

New media and deregulation have changed the dynamics of business, but they can't change personalities. Some people will be forever creative, indulging fantasies in storytelling and games; others retain business heads, managing balance sheets and compliance issues, and keeping an eye out for attractive acquisitions.

Creative people with the highest marketable value excel in their creative discipline but match it with a business approach – people like Steven Spielberg, a genius who knows how he wants to run his business, SKG Dreamworks. It is, according to its website, the 'artist-friendly' studio producing movies to inspire worldwide audiences.

What goes around comes around: performing wasn't enough for Chaplin
Source: Historical Archive

Charlie Chaplin was an artist who wanted to control his own destiny, understanding that to do so he must complement artistry with business acumen. When his employers, the Hollywood studios, fussed about bankrolling his overbudget productions, Chaplin felt creatively constrained – even though overbudget and beyond-deadline films hardly show the most prescient business forethought. With the support of other performers and producers, Chaplin formed United Artists, a studio in which talent would be respected and in ultimate control. Creativity would no longer be inhibited by the constraints of accountants who had little understanding of the creative process. 'I might as well have been a lone factory worker asking

General Motors for a raise,' Chaplin (1964) said of his days toiling for the large studios. 'Exhibitors were rugged merchants in those days and to them films were merchandise costing so much a yard.' Seems ironic, considering the importance of merchandise to Chaplin's successors almost a century on.

But at the time, the film was all, and even the bosses agreed. Adolph Zukor, president and founder of Paramount, who at one point considered joining Chaplin's United Artists, supported performers in their battle to wrest control, but said creativity must be countered with a business approach. He told Chaplin:

> You have every right to get the full benefit of your efforts because you are artists! You create! It is you that the people come to see … You are creative at one end of the business, I am creative at the other. What could be sweeter?

Businesspeople and creative people, if they are not one and the same in the Chaplin or Spielberg mould, should at least act as one. Businesses where the creative elements and the business side are separate have a harder task than those in which there is a mutual sense of what is fundamentally resonant, salient and in touch with what audiences want.

When artists have their heads without being managed or thinking about audience, they attract either a small audience or critical scorn, or even both. Often, they go bankrupt along the way.

The European film industry, for example, contains many educated, arty practitioners making rather tragic stories that they, and only they, would like to explore and in which too few others are interested. The stories are richer in characterization than plot, narrative is displaced by theme, and much effort is spent on beautiful cinematography at the expense of attention to script. This, of course, is a cynical simplification, but it's probably true to say that European film concentrates excessively on art to the detriment of the business side, and that thoughts of an audience are secondary to the concerns of bringing an auteur's imagination to the screen.

From time to time, usually in comedy, there's a success. A movie made for a comparatively low budget, which hits a resonant note and achieves critical and commercial success. These achievements, being rare, gain disproportionate levels of critical interest. They come round about once every two years. These movies have much more structure than their failing dramatic contemporaries. And structure is something that audiences understand. Far from failing to be original, the creatives have examined a basic business tenet – audiences seldom buy things they do not understand.

Creative businesses such as film, television, music and publishing are ultimately in the fashion business. Fashion can have an enormous commercial and creative impact for a short period of time, transferring over a number of media before falling into the creative graveyard. This is not what we seek. The best creative content not only makes a strong initial impact; it endures and finds new audiences through the generations.

In the midst of 1970s glam rock, the Bay City Rollers sold millions of records, tartan T-shirts, scarfs and three-quarter-length trousers that would never see the light of day again. Neither would the music. 'Shang-a-Lang' plays on few credible radio stations today. Yet at their height, with ten top-ten hits in the UK, the Scottish boy band were big before the term 'boy band' had been coined. They transferred across media as far as they could, but largely found they couldn't (their own television series, for example, exposed their limitations as broadcasters). Fatally, the band's members didn't own the intellectual property in their recordings, the record company made all the money, and when they disbanded they had to find an honest living outside the music business.

That's fashion that doesn't endure. One has to take the money and run. Far better to produce sticky content that can transfer down the ages as well as across media.

Today, you can be a one-hit wonder on your own terms. You may still need a record company to get into the charts, but then the charts are a child of the record companies. For how long, though, before there's a new measure of musical success?

THE HITS BUSINESS

Hits businesses are about failure as much as they are about success. Everyone dreams of success, but few achieve it. Like business in general, the ratio of failure to success is high. Most of the projects submitted to be made into a book, film or record are rejected out of hand. And the ones on which publishers take a punt seldom go on to make large amounts of money.

Creating the hits requires creative judgement as well as an assessment of business risk. This is the ultimate portfolio business.

Creating the hits requires creative judgement as well as an assessment of business risk.

In the music industry each year, where more than 10,000 records are released, a few hundred make it on to radio playlists – which are essential if they are to have any hope of success – and then a couple of dozen turn into global sellers. A handful of hit records pay for the thousands of unsuccessful releases.

Media consultant John Cummings of Hawkpoint Partners likens it to a beetle race, rather than a horse race: 'A lot of projects just stop, or go backwards, or rest for a while. Managing in the media is all about things that are not going to plan, rather than the things that are.'

The hits business is an amalgam of fashion and science. A scientist, like an artist, immerses his or herself in the subject, lives it daily, and believes in its importance to the extent that it is often the absorbing focus of their life. Fashion succeeds when an artist creates something new that engages with enough people – notably, the right kind of people – to snowball through a section of society. As in the pharmaceutical business, the scientists of creative business manage a portfolio of projects, anticipating that the few will pay for the development of the many.

But to create a hit, you have to engage with a large number of people, and make more money than you spend.

The Darwinian portfolio approach, producing many so that the few survive, often leaves audiences with the impression that standards are pretty low. If they think some of the stuff they hear and see is bad, then they should witness some of the content that never makes it to publication. Now, with lower barriers to entry and many more outlets, a lot more lower-quality material sees the light of day. But there's no real relationship between quality and quotas – as more material is produced, some of it is good, much of it less so. It has always been thus.

Having so much more content available generally means that somewhere, all the time, there's something available for everyone. The democratization of media – more people can now get their artistic endeavours in front of an audience – means that talent that previously would have been undiscovered now has a greater chance of making it to the surface.

THE FALLACY OF THE GOLDEN AGE

The doomsayers condemn democratization as a lowering of standards. They point to the increasing volume of apparent rubbish that blights television and cinema screens or blasts out of their radios.

The appeal is for a return to the golden age. A time when a few television stations served up quality documentaries and dramas without bad language. When pop music was raucous, yes, but at least it had a good tune. And when films were original and entertaining – not relentless sequels of a former success or formulaic Hollywood shoot-em-ups. In short, a time like it was when parents were teenagers.

Being 15 or 16, when one starts to cut free from the constraints of childhood, is, for most people, a memorable, intense time. Knowing this, some sticky storytellers attempt to match content with the corresponding period in their audience's life when they were in their mid-teens. It's a particularly useful wheeze in the advertising industry. Choosing the right backing music for a commercial can make or break it. Returning to the target market's teenage years to find a track is almost assured to tingle nerves. And even if the music doesn't numerically match the teenage years, an evocative tune from a period with which the audience would like to identify but can't because age prevents it can do just as well.

Right now, in the early years of the new century, there's not too much call in the movies for rock 'n' roll tracks of the 1950s. It's just too long ago to capture an emotion among a large enough audience from the cinema-going audience. The clarion call for nostalgia of the 1950s came in the 1970s and early 1980s. The *Happy Days* years. When films like the *Blues Brothers*, *National Lampoon's Animal House* and, a little later, *American Graffiti* rocked the cinemas. Nostalgia evokes a golden age, and a golden age is what we used to like.

The audience of the early days of rock 'n' roll are now in their 60s and 70s. The Saga market. Some are profitable silver-surfers with disposable incomes, but who spend much of it on holidays, insurance and, when online, relatively simple interactive tools like email and, possibly, financial tracking. But many are state pensioners who are not wired, connected or digitized in any form, many of whom never will be.

But still the idea of a golden age is a fallacy. More is better because we are not compelled to consume the paucity on offer or do nothing.

It's hard to imagine that the television hits from a generation ago, for example, are qualitatively any better than their counterparts today. Are *Kojak*, *Charlies Angels* and *Starsky and Hutch* head and shoulders above *ER*, *Sex in the City* or the *West Wing*? Those who complain that there's nothing on television worth watching these days, or any new music worth listening to, clearly aren't paying attention. Their complaints are borne out of assumptions, not facts, a desire to criticize rather than contribute.

And people do like to complain about content in ways they would never do about services they have paid for directly. They complain about music they don't like and would never buy, about free-to-air television pro-grammes they don't watch funded by advertising, and about the content of newspapers they don't buy and won't read. When one's reputation is so strong that people know what you're about without consuming your story, that is arguably one measure of success. How many people do you know who have very firm opinions about a newspaper and then appear to know what's in it? How do these people know if they don't read it? Partly because they read summaries in other papers, or see extracts on television, or they can't resist reading bits of other people's paper on the train or the bus. They might not have bought it, and may never buy it, but they read and see and they count.

When, in 1993, the BBC dramatized Hanif Kureishi's novel *The Buddha of Surburbia*, they stuck what was thought to be a minority-interest drama on BBC2 on a midweek evening without too much fanfare. It attracted a modest audience, until red-top national paper the *Sun* criticized the BBC for showing seedy, explicit, almost pornographic content. The BBC's phone lines went into overdrive, with people outraged at the BBC's decision to show such unsuitable material. Many callers hadn't seen the show, but lots more people latched on to *The Buddha of Suburbia* because of the seem-ingly negative publicity and the prospect of a hot night in front of the box. Ratings soared. The following morning, the *Sun* abandoned its supposed outrage to have a bit of a laugh instead. 'You dirty lot', it chastised.

It's too easy to suggest that everyone who criticizes media content and harks back to a golden era is an older, prudish figure finding it difficult to adapt to a multiband age. But the cry, 'It's not as good as it used to be' is, by definition, uttered by people who recall how it used to be. Criticism from the young is of a different nature, usually along the lines of 'There's nothing there for me.'

Those harking back to a golden age do so because they remember the stories and the music that appeared to be addressing them. And it was presented on a technology that was new and exciting. Vinyl records. Television. Now those media have changed, it appears that it no longer addresses them. That confuses the medium with the message.

HITS HAVE ATTITUDE

Creating a real hit – in financial and critical terms – demands an attitude as much as a great idea. Attitude is about knowing one's story, knowing the audience, and then knowing what to do to get it delivered. That needs business judgement in the producing organization.

It's often assumed, sometimes rightly, that creative people and business-people are two breeds that don't get on. They care about different things. But it doesn't have to be that way. In Hollywood, and in much of the music business, you won't find many people who aren't deeply interested in making money. Back to Charlie Chaplin, the Brit who made it big in Hollywood. He was fanatically interested in ensuring his art made money, his 50% share in United Artists focusing the mind on the relation between costs of production and box-office receipts. There's an undisputed heritage in creativity making profit, and everyone along the value chain, from artists to distributors, can benefit.

The hits with the biggest value aren't one-off wonders. What one really needs to create is hit property – something that can last many years, and that can be transferred across media, earning money all the way.

Hits that don't have what it takes to become hit properties still have a value – but only for a while. If you're an artist, being a one-hit wonder or having only the occasional hit doesn't fulfil the whole dream. Artists seek longevity, basking in the glory of the first hit, despondent when the second doesn't arrive. Nevertheless, even one hit could become profitable if it's a sticky one. At the very least, it can lead to a lifetime's demand as an act on a cruise liner.

Non-sticky hits abound. Often, they have more to do with timing than talent. Many pop records are not that good, produced in the hope of finding the few successes among the many failures. Yet somehow, they find resonance with an audience at a particular time. They may get on a radio playlist somewhere by finding a sympathetic ear in contrast to the deaf ones at other stations. Picked up once, they gather moss and generate enough of a roll to sell well. They are Joe Dolce's *Shaddap You Face* and the Saint Winifred's Girls' School Choir, both of which took the top spot in the UK singles charts once, never to return thereafter. Their value today is as nostalgia. But then again, not all nostalgia is in demand. It's just old content, gathering dust in the archives.

Manufacturing a singular hit, rather than a hit property, depends on exploiting the characteristics of the medium for which one is producing. In music, it's about providing something intensely personal to individuals, even though it may be bought by millions of people. It is heard on an individual basis, and means something different to everyone. Radio listening evokes similar personal feelings: 'It's just for me.'

Successful movies are diversions, taking audiences away from wherever they are, transporting them away from the everyday world into a story that has little to do with everyday life. Audiences escape, have a short holiday, then return to their daily lives.

Newspapers are almost solely about attitude, rather than information or news. Most newspapers are run by rather unpleasant people (usually men), and their publications are more about what they are against rather than about what they are for. (The exception being the *Financial Times*, where we used to work and which, for the record, is run by fine, upstanding gentlemen of the highest calibre.)

THE TRANSFER OF MUSIC ACROSS MEDIA

Music isn't what it used to be. It's better – with more variety and choice. And, because of the plethora of ways to hear it cheaply, music is always available, wherever you go.

Even ten years ago, that simply wasn't true. Music stores may have been able to sell you most types of music, or at least put in an order for anything obscure. But on radio, with limited spectrum, the number of formats offered was correspondingly small. Most stations played popular types of music – top 40, adult rock, middle-of-the-road. In the USA, with relaxed regulation, a station could play country music one day, then open up as a rock and roll station the next if the owner thought it more profitable. Hearing what you liked depended on living within range of a transmitter playing your kind of music.

Today in the UK, there are about 60 channels of music on Sky Digital's television platform alone, offering just about every type of music whenever the listener wants it. Years ago, audiences bought tickets for concerts and shows, or sat around the piano making their own entertainment. Today, they download whatever they want to hear in a box and plug it into their ears and annoy other people around them.

But music isn't just there to be heard. It's almost the perfect type of content for transfer across media – to watch, sing along to, and share. And it's addictive.

Into Britney Spears? Buy the record, see the show, get the T-shirt, and wear the 'Baby One More Time' wristwatch (but have a lot of back-up batteries: it just chews through them).

The best transfers work, as always, when the characteristics of the medium are used to tell the right bit of the story. Dance music, for example, has – to the ears of much of an entire generation – an addictive beat. So addictive, in fact, that some people are known to listen to it during the day. (This is, of course, the kind of dance music that has a high number of beats per minute, as opposed to, say, a military two-step or foxtrot.) This kind of music doesn't need a narrative structure for most of its transition across media, so it doesn't work too well on, say, television, where it's hard to make a long show out of people at turntables or jumping up and down with their vests off. In the 1980s, *The Hitman and Her* took such a show from a nightclub and showed it on television at 3 am – club-throwing-out time. It wasn't a major hit because nightclubs provide an experience, not a story, and experiences are difficult to recreate without an element of interaction. Recording the music and broadcasting it on television recreates sounds and lights but little else of the nightclub experience.

Live music works because of structure as much as the music and performance itself – the warm-up, main act and encore. A three-act play. The beginning, middle and end. With variations of pace and delivery, bands match and manipulate the mood of the audience through the evening. When performing, artists deliver a different part of their story than that in their recorded music. Big acts fill stadiums in a show rather than a concert. Appearing is only one bit of the event: lasers, costumes, choreography and support musicians are elements of each set. This is a social occasion, fulfilling community, and is at one end of the experience of musical art. At the other is a demand for music 'unplugged'.

Musical success is a fairy tale, much like sport; a meritocracy where the poorest can rise to the top if they have talent, commitment and a dream. Bryan McFadden of boy band Westlife, in the sleeve notes to hit CD 'Coast to Coast,' thanks his manager and record company 'for making this fairy-tale come true in front of our very eyes'.

Eminem isn't just a rap singer. He's a story. With his mask and chainsaw, his foul-mouthed lyrics, and deprived childhood, he is every parent's nightmare. That's popular music. Jerry Lee Lewis and Bill Haley frightened parents of the 1950s in a similar fashion.

The BBC spent many years suppressing pop music on radio, despite the fact that there was a known market for it, and commercial competition was prohibited by law until as late as 1973. Pirate radio, broadcast from ships anchored outside UK jurisdiction, filled the gap, with sound quality so poor that even good music sounded bad. The BBC was protecting its channel, its position as a powerful patron of music, and its own cultural delusion that it alone knew what kinds of music were and were not appropriate for the British public.

Before the BBC, there was very little in the way of commercial music in the UK. Music halls were about the limit of the hit machine, with the most popular tunes making it into sheet music to be sung round the piano. Along came the BBC, and by the mid-1930s, it was the biggest employer of musicians in the country. Recording technologies did exist for home consumption of music – the phonograph being invented in 1882 – but records contributed only a fraction of revenues to the Performing Rights Society. The BBC provided the major source of income.

That's not to say music wasn't a popular pastime. Like storytelling, music unites communities and always has. But only technology universalizes music in a standard, original form – before recording equipment was invented, no two performances were ever the same, and its introduction baffled audiences. Why would anyone want to listen to old music when live performances are much more satisfying?

With the advent of broadcasting, professional music reached millions of people for the first time and records brought the consumer's personal choice of music into the home. In the UK, the first full year of regular broadcasting, 1923, coincided with the arrival of the dance craze (not hip hop or drum 'n' bass, but something one did in the late afternoons or early evenings, often with tea and cake). Within a year, the BBC broadcast dance music every night of the week, which frankly appeared unseemly in a country that would not allow the purchase of alcohol in the afternoons until the end of the millennium. In an early example of cross-media integration, the *Radio Times* reproduced photographs of how to do the Charleston for those who wanted to try it at home (see illustration overleaf).

But creating hits through cross-media promotion was more problematic. The BBC, being publicly funded, with a commitment to educate, entertain and inform, didn't exist to help other people sell records.

So early on, vocal numbers performed by bands on BBC radio were banned to prevent recort promotion. At one point, the BBC removed microphones from band leaders to stop the public finding out what they were listening to. The music, they deemed, was the important thing, not everything else to do with it – such as title, track and artist. Broadcasting existed for people to listen and learn, not for them subsequently to go out and buy records that would then take up time when they could be listening to further broadcasts (even though for much of the time the airwaves remained dead).

By taking tight control, the BBC argued that it delivered 'the true democratization of music' (Scannell and Cardiff, 1990) – everyone, everywhere could enjoy the best performances in the world. They soon gave in to listeners' protests and reinstated announcements, and, creating the first pundits, hired announcers to provide context to programmes. Control, though, remained in the hands of the few, and the subjective opinion of

Best foot forward: the BBC's Charleston guide for audiences trying it out at home.

Source: Getty Images/Hulton Archive

important decision-makers determined the success of music. In 1936, the BBC's director of programmes, Cecil Graves, deemed crooning (a style in which the performer sings close to the microphone, personified by Bing Crosby and copied by Robbie Williams) to be 'a particularly odious form of singing' that must not be broadcast.

Bing, of course, was unable to resort to distributing his own material and had the good fortune to live in the USA, where commercial broadcasting predated that of a much weaker public sector. Had he faced a broadcasting boycott today, he would have discovered that there are many more ways to get his music to the masses. As it is, Bing Crosby downloads on the Web have been minimal.

Technology means we can all be producers or, even better, stars. If we want to retain our independence and create music free from commercial influences, it's not only possible, it's something of which many musicians are proud.

But equally, if we want to be widely heard, broadcast or narrowcast, then the thousands if not millions of entirely new hours of airtime have to be filled. There are audiences there just waiting. The trick is finding them.

CHECKLIST: CREATING HIT PROPERTY

- Know thy subject. Not just a bit. Be thoroughly immersed in it. Be thoughtful about it.
- Think about the delivery of your creation – the environment in which it is consumed.
- Produce the content that you want to produce – but be guided by others in your collaborative art.
- Allow one person to have overall creative direction.
- Businesspeople know what they are doing – great ones help deliver the maximum audience.
- If maximizing audience is your aim, package elements in which many people will be interested, and deliver it better than anyone else.
- If your content isn't the best in the market, then schedule or distribute it differently. If it's the best, go head to head.
- Stick to what you're good at. If you don't really know how to do something in a different medium, then don't waste a lot of money and energy proving it.
- To transfer your hit across media, hire an expert in your target medium.
- Hits are about fashion as much as excellence – luck plays a part.
- It's a beetle race – you have more chance of winning if you back a lot of beetles.

'… what we do at Disney is very simple … Above all, we tell stories in the hope that they will entertain, inform and engage.'

Michael Eisner, CEO, Disney Corporation

Here's a paradox. The world's greatest storyteller, knocking around now for the best part of a century, successfully transfers its stories across film, television, books, toys, theme parks and ocean-going liners. Then along comes the Internet, a whole new opportunity for storytelling magic, and the ball is dropped. Just why was that?

Despite an absence of massive blockbuster hits since the *Lion King* and *Toy Story*, and the trauma of a misjudged Internet strategy, Disney builds on its storytelling heritage, transferring hits across media. When Disney gets new stories right, fresh characters are welcomed by families the world over. When it gets it wrong, the new content franchise fizzles out (such as *Dinosaurs* in 2000).

What began in 1928 with an animated mouse is one of the world's greatest media companies with more than 100,000 employees. In addition to the famous film studios and distributors, embracing Buena Vista, Miramax and Touchstone, and theme parks (with Disneylands from California to Tokyo), Disney's empire includes shops, publication companies, a cable TV network and US broadcaster ABC, an eponymous TV channel, and teams in the US national hockey league (the Mighty Ducks) and major-league baseball (Anaheim Angels). In short, Disney is big and wants to be bigger.

Making the Mickey

The pitter-patter of tiny feet first arrived five years after Walt Disney, along with his brother Roy, formed the company in 1923. *Fantasia* and *Pinocchio* followed *Mickey Mouse*, but the first full-length animated feature, *Snow White*, brought the most fame, becoming the highest grossing film of its time in its first year. It took $8.5 million at a time when a child's cinema ticket cost ten cents.

Walt Disney adored stories, taking fairy stories and making them his own. A genius who dreamed big dreams, he was a consummate collaborator, involving many people in the storytelling process. While developing the Pirates of the Caribbean ride (which is still a major attraction at Disney resorts and, in a new example of transferability across media, is in development as a movie), Walt called everyone together – from janitors to resort executives – to discuss why the attraction just wasn't working out. A cleaner suggested that fireflies would complete the magic. Live lightening bugs were imported – until such a time when technology improved and their jobs were taken by mechanical flies. Walt awarded the cleaner a bonus, the ride was considered complete, and it continues to be one of the most popular rides.

Storytelling reinvented

Disney embarked on new projects in the 1980s following the arrival of chief executive Michael Eisner. Theme parks were reinvigorated, and new rides devised, based around new blockbuster movies. To go to Disneyworld is one thing, but to go to Disneyworld and stay in a Disney hotel is the way to capture the whole experience. Ask a kid. Who do you want to serve you breakfast before a day in the park? A geeky 17-year-old or Pluto?

The Disney Corporation changed strategy in the 1980s, releasing its film library on sell-through video. Previously, the studio had stuck to a seven-year cycle of theatrical releases, raking in box-office revenues from each new generation of tots. If it could work for *Snow White* in every decade since the 1930s, why change a winning formula?

The switch to video worked. These are sticky stories, which children watch over and over again – making videos attractive to own and good value. As scenes and lines are learned, and songs are sung and sung again, a Disney story takes on a life – earning licence fees from games and toys and books. The story is a franchise, which cross-promotes other Disney businesses. Characters sell toys, movies, attractions at the theme parks, promote holidays, and encourage visits to Disney stores.

Disney hopes to create stories which transfer across media and through time, and spends major marketing dollars on strong stories. 2001 movie *Monsters Inc* cost about $100 million to produce, and then a further $175 million in marketing, though Disney's partnerships with brands such as McDonald's, Hasbro toys, Kraft and Pepsi recouped some of the costs. Not many films achieve box office revenues of more than $100 million, and analysts' expectations that *Monsters Inc* would bring in around $200 million in the US were soon beaten. By May 2002, the film was just outside the all-time movie top 20, with worldwide revenues in excess of half a billion dollars. That's big – but it is only as the film moves through the distribution chain of film, video and TV rights, and other related sales that Disney realizes the full potential its investment.

Monsters Inc – keeps Disney in its core happiness business. The company is dependent upon the imagination of creative people and the commitment and hard work of tens of thousands of its 'cast members' to deliver a high-quality, consistent story experience. It reflects in a company training manual:

> For all its success, the Disney theme show is quite a fragile thing. It takes one contradiction, one out of place stimulus, to negate a particular moment's experience … tack up a felt tip brown paper sign that says Keep Out … place a touch of astro turf here … add a surly employee there … it really doesn't take too much to upset it all.

To keep the Disney story focused, each employee has an internal or external client to be kept happy.

Disney goes digital

It's 1996 and the world is talking Internet. It's the next big medium, and Disney has to be there. This is territory different from Disney's origins. Film-making is owned by storytellers, and the medium in which the story is told, whilst important, is secondary. Unlike broadcasting, where programmes were invented after television, cinema was made for film. Walt Disney and his company knew how to create content for existing media – cinema was around for decades before Mickey Mouse.

But the Internet demanded the creation of new content that was not necessarily linear narrative. In common with many companies at the time, Disney initially stuck to brochureware, launching Disney.com – a promotional site for Disney products.

At the start of 1999, Disney and Infoseek, a search engine, began the Go Network, a portal. 'Portal' was the buzz word of 1999, just as much as 'Internet' was four years earlier – the way to go if you're serious about Web strategy. The intention was to compete with the likes of Yahoo! and AOL. Disney soon bought out Infoseek, combining all its Internet holdings in the Go Network and starting a tracking stock, the Disney Internet Group.

Go.com initially incorporated Infoseek's search capabilities with the best of Disney's content, together with personalized features, email, shopping and community areas. Describing the venture at the time, CEO Michael Eisner said that Go would 'serve as a central hub through which people can gain access to every business and every form of information and entertainment that Disney offers' (abcnews.com, 1999) This is more than just telling a story.

Following disappointing user figures and revenues, Disney abandoned its portal in January 2001. Go went, as did the Internet tracker. Branded websites remain, making it easier for audiences to find what they're looking for. It's not much of a guess to think that checking out *Toy Story*'s website would involve the words 'toy story' – going through Go only frustrated the audience.

The lessons

One might not know the exact words in the mission statement, but most people could have a stab at guessing what Disney Corp stands for. Family values. Dreams. Great stories. Cartoons, perhaps, or adventures. It's safe, it's fun, it's American, it's Mickey Mouse.

Now try the same with Go.com. Ask around: who owns Go? what is Go? what does Go do? If you bury the gems, the brand names – Disney, ABC, ESPN – under a generic word on which money has to be spent trying to forge ownership, you're facing an uphill battle on a mountain of your own making.

Go's strategy was never clear, morphing from the brochureware of Disney.com, through a portal stage, then broadening into a general entertainment site. There was a desire to make money, and despite the fact that few Internet businesses had learned how to do it, there was an overriding fear that unless one made massive investments, the company would fall behind. A landgrab was made, building sites to keep ahead of both the competition and the Internet learning curve, and then a clarion call made for people to come visit.

In essence, Disney didn't stick to its knitting. This is a company that knows how to minimize the downside, but crucially, when it came to an innovative new medium, didn't. This is a company that knows how to extract maximum value from synergies across disparate parts of its business. With the right intentions, it tried this with the Web but misjudged demand. This is a business that is adept at managing tensions between creative collaborators, but found that the creators of ideas and the Internet operational managers could not be reconciled. Most of all, this is a company that knows its audience and what they want. They wanted great stories, told with imagination, and they continue to do so today. They may want an aggregator of content, and they may want it from someone with an unusual URL. But they don't want that from Disney.

From Disney, they demand great new stories, exciting ways of interacting with those stories, and the knowledge that whoever they talk to, the chances are they will have heard the same story.

REFERENCES

Abcnews.com, 'Disney tries new web feat', abcnews.com, June 1999.

Charles Chaplin, *My Autobiography*, Penguin, 1964.

Scannell, P. and Cardiff, D., *A Social History of Broadcasting*, Blackwell, 1990.

MAKING IT REAL: DRAMA AND INTERACTION

4

61

'You only use 12% of your brain.
   Mind if we play with the rest?'

Majestic, Electronic Arts game

Majestic is a horror of a game that plays you.

It knows where you live. It rings you at two in the morning. It's a story that jumps from the box to get you.

This is the new drama. A drama you live and play, not watch. You are at the centre of the story, and it's going to interact with your life. It's scary stuff.

Majestic, and other games of its genre, heralds the new type of storytelling. Out of the proscenium arch of the theatre, breaking the walnut panelling around the television set, drama is no longer a passive experience.

Interactive games, especially those played with Internet connections, fulfil two complementary functions. As stories, they achieve what stories have always achieved: entertainment, education and empathy. And as businesses, they can become hit properties – or, as with many creative businesses, fail spectacularly.

Majestic, made by Electronic Arts, wasn't entirely successful online, failing to reach sufficient subscribers, although the CD version holds more promise. Online, it capitalized on the Internet's interactivity and immersiveness. But the story was episodic – customers had to wait a month between chapters. And that's not in keeping with the immediacy of the medium. (By contrast, Electronic Arts' 'persistent universe' game, Ultima, keeps on running even when the player isn't actively playing the game. In the first half of 2002, it had more than 200,000 subscribers paying $10 a month.)

THE COMMON THREADS OF DRAMA

Drama creates worlds, worlds that may be fantastic or realistic, that have their own rules, sensitivities, characters and settings. We like enclosed worlds – prisons, spaceships, rolling rural idylls, ganglands. They are places that the audience recognizes as a world, and in which unusual events occur in a self-contained space as we watch.

Until now, we've viewed such drama from a distance. Through a TV, or cinema screen, passively.

Now traditional narrative drama is under threat. Unless the story is transferable across media – the potential to become the hit property, rather than just the hit – it will be ephemeral. There will still be countless opportunities for hits within a single medium. They will be the one-hit wonders of their genre.

These one-hit wonders are to be honoured if that is the extent of their ambition – as are those pieces of hit content that succeed in a single medium. Some stories simply won't transfer across media – just like dance music on television.

Today's one hit wonders generally sell less well than even half a generation ago. In television, a successful drama series could reasonably expect to achieve 15 million viewers in the UK in 1990. Today, a good one achieves nearer eight million. Film success requires fewer people past the box office (higher ticket prices generate the same volumes of revenues) because theatrical sales are not as financially important as the cumulative audience reached as the story passes down the distribution chain. More than 80% of film revenues are likely to come from sources other than ticket sales.

Today's measure of success is not just the raw numbers in a single medium. It is the sales potential across many media. And that depends on transferability.

The measure of success is no longer just the raw numbers in a single medium. It is the sales potential across many media. And that depends on transferability.

TECHNOLOGY BEGETS REALITY

Whether the story is new or old, a historical piece or the retelling of a favourite, the change that technology brings is the feeling of immediacy, involvement or 'liveness' – even when its delivery patently isn't live, as in the movies. Stories that make the audience feel like they are part of it may be told in real time, or may have special effects that are so realistic that they engender a feeling of being there.

Reality now extends beyond narrative drama into many forms of entertainment, sometimes to the detriment of traditional ways of telling stories. Old linear forms, still quite relevant, now have to fight for creative resources, access to distribution, and share of the audience's attention.

This has happened, for example, in documentary programming. Instead of filming someone as they learn to drive, the story becomes drama, and the participants, for a time, are celebrities. Dramatic structures replace the documentary form, and it morphs into entertainment. Drama-documentaries, docusoaps. Anything pure in form has to fight to survive. Travel books turn into adventure stories, novels sometimes so shallow in narrative description that they could almost be film scripts. That's not to say this is necessarily good or bad; it certainly helps transferability, and it certainly appears more dramatic.

Here's an example from television. By the mid-1990s, game shows were almost completely dead in the USA. In Europe, some survived into the early evening, but they were slowly sliding into the dearth that is daytime television. Games were a form in decline.

Dying forms are revived by drama – and stories. When UK production house Celdor devised *Who Wants to be a Millionaire?*, new life was breathed into decay. This Lazarus-like resurrection reinvented TV games formats almost single-handedly.

At the start of the new century, *Who Wants to be a Millionaire?* was a massive global programme franchise, adapting to local markets with country-specific questions and domestic presenters, but maintaining international brand consistency. Travel the world to watch *Millionaire* and you might not understand a word that's being said in foreign tongues, but you will certainly know what you're watching and whether the question was answered correctly.

The game show in which the host was the star, entertaining the studio audience and those at home with a barrage of gags and much less of a quiz, is sinking towards its grave. New television games have a strong dramatic structure where the audience – who can participate, in the studio and at home – look into the eyes of a person as they make tantalizing decisions. *Millionaire*, *The Weakest Link*, and no doubt newer shows that will become hit properties, share common characteristics:

- They have the feeling of being live – but they aren't.
- Elements of story – we get to know the contestants and sometimes their families.
- Strong dramatic structure.
- Music and lighting which creates drama.
- Consistent branding worldwide – the set, the music, the logo – creates a franchise.
- They are interactive – viewers join in, even when they're not joining in. Shouting at the screen is the first rung on the ladder of the interactive franchise, which can extend to Internet games, gaming machines in bars, and board games.

Reality and drama are base elements for the future of entertainment. Games without drama, games where most of the audience is a passive participant, rather than an interactive one – even if interaction is as simple as shouting at the screen – are not transferable. No longer are games about watching others having a nice time just being there.

Nice is OK, especially if it wins a substantial pot of money. But it's much more dramatic if even the bad guys, the people you think shouldn't even be allowed on television, can get away with the booty. That's a great story. We like stories.

These shows, based on drama, interaction and live-ness, have the characteristics of extendability. They may not last forever in the big league – most game shows have a life at the top of about four or five years before the audience wants to hear a different story (they then start slipping into less competitive slots) – but the producers can find markets for the content in many media during that window. The audience can play the game at home using interactive television, partake of the game on the Internet or in a bar on a gaming machine, or play in the old-economy world by buying the board game or book. The BBC even provided instructions of how to make an Anne Robinson scary mask on its website. When you're a scary mask, you're sticky.

THE DRAMA OF LIVE EVENTS

A more connected world brings stories to life. When we're wired, stories are accessible all the time, wherever we go. Like Majestic, the game – or, more pertinently, the news.

Since the dawn of broadcasting, world events have driven the penetration of technology. Sales of television sets rose dramatically before the coronation of Queen Elizabeth in 1953.

It's no accident that journalists refer to news events as 'stories'. In the perverse way that is the journalist's lot, even the most dreadful events are good stories. Anyone who has worked in a newsroom will recall the thrill of hearing of some disaster and be appalled to catch themselves thinking 'good story'. Bad stories are good stories because they are so easy to do – and so eagerly consumed.

Yet technology has not changed the manner in which news stories are told. It has, though, made them more accessible, more likely to be personal to the reader, and often more intrusive. Big news events, the start of the Gulf War, the terrorist attacks on New York and Washington, come to us live. As they do, audiences gravitate towards the media that explain live dramas best – the narrative news of television, the fuller context of newspapers, the reflection and intimacy of radio. The Web provides updates and a terrific source of classified, statistical and community information – but it is used to extend and personalize the story, not to replace the live drama. At the same time, technology allows audiences to opt out of news, sharing fewer events. There's so much more of it, but so much more of all other content too.

News may be continuous, but its presentation in story format is changed little by technology. We like stories more than raw facts. Someone who knows about these things needs to help us sift and make sense. The intermediary is not dead, not dying, not even a bit unwell. It's just the role that's different, a bit more dramatic, and the stories a bit more live – or presented as if they were live.

Delving back in history, the format of television news 'packages', for example, told a story, spiced it with personality, and presented it as live as the technology of the day allowed. The package originated in a manifesto written by Edward Jay Epstein, the producer of the US Humphrey-Brinkley show in 1962, around the time that lightweight cameras allowed journalists to get around a bit more, permitting a faster response between an event and its broadcast. Epstein recommended the production of packages of between one and a half and three minutes in length, with the reporter speaking to camera at the scene – the appearance of liveness, even if not broadcast live – and reporting emotions as much as facts. Stories, said Epstein, should have a rising cadence and a falling cadence, and should be mini-dramas in their space.

This format became a world standard and is identifiable in thousands of news programmes even today. Continuous news programmes constantly flit live to the scene, and reporters now introduce their own recorded packages of film and interviews. The reports are extended with interviews with the presenter back in the studio – 'two-ways' – journalists interviewing journalists. Stories form a starting point for interaction with the audience – phone-ins, emails, polling. But the format of the story remains as it has for 40 years – a three-minute package, narrated by a reporter, sitting within longer, more frequent, or even continuous programming.

It is similar in sport, where technological developments have fundamentally changed its financing (bringing more money in), but also its organization and structure. If you take the king's shilling, you have to be prepared to live by another's rules.

Sport is a dramatic form in itself, told in bite-sized lumps – individual games – that are part of a larger meal – a season, league or tournament. They have characters called players, goodies (Arthur Ashe, Gary Lineker), baddies (John McEnroe, all referees), sets (pitches and courts) and music (majorettes, brass bands at half time). Sport is gladiatorial entertainment. It is best told live.

As with pantomime, the nature of sport – as opposed to the reporting of sport – succumbs to social changes, as much as technological ones. Soccer is a minority sport in the USA because, despite its pacy nature, it has a relatively low strike rate. Even though in much of the rest of the world grown men can be reduced to sobbing wrecks by 22 men chasing a leather, air-filled bag, the prospect of a nil-nil score line excites few American males. It took its introduction on television to bring it any kind of profile, leading to the USA hosting the World Cup in 1994.

If there is a perfect sport for television, then snooker would have to come close. Its green baize table fits almost exactly on to the screen, and a tournament with 32 players and several hundred games can easily fill whole weeks of schedules. It's also cheap and popular, which makes it very attractive to multi-channel platform owners. You can bet on it, get to know the players through background briefings, interact in chat rooms, play it in bars. It's transferable.

Those same characteristics have never helped snooker's older cousin, billiards, which has never achieved the same televisual success – though it did change one of its rules in the 1980s to speed up the game (players can only pot the red from the black spot three consecutive times, not five, these days). Television producers didn't rush forward with lucrative contracts in response, and the game is dying along with its aging players (although the audience of www.billiards.com – with 'billiards' best discussion forum' and instructional items to improve your game – may wish to disagree).

And only places that enjoy a leisurely pace of life (India, West Indies, parts of Yorkshire) seem to tolerate cricket, where games last five days and can still be a draw. Explain cricket to an American and they'll look at you as if you're completely off your head.

Yet technology is being used to create drama and stories, even in cricket. Previously, only the most loyal of fans would follow their team as they travelled the country or the world. Few would understand the strengths and weaknesses of each individual player, or be able to recite their batting or bowling averages. Television and radio, being limited in hours available for each sport, and the desire to reach a sizable audience, could not hope to cover all but the most important of matches.

Now, new camera angles, computer animation, and the ability to get closer to the centre of the action with pictures and sound have created a more intimate relationship between viewers and audience. The players are becoming characters, giving interviews within minutes of leaving the field, explaining the strategy – how they are plotting, thinking and, hopefully, leading the story towards a happy ending. UK commercial broadcaster Channel 4 has breathed new life into cricket coverage and is educating the audience as well as creating drama, rather than passively filming a day's leisurely activity on the field. Want to find out more? The Web provides the depth and the opportunity to interact, to be part of a revived, more youthful cricketing community. Live drama has been brought to cricket. Some would scarcely think it possible.

We are now so used to events being live and accessible that anything that is recorded, or old, or just hard to get at has a much lower value. The excitement of watching sport is that the drama unfolds before your eyes. None of the players, officials or audience knows how the narrative is going to develop. All understand the structure, the rules of the game, but the outcome and how it will be reached are unknown, simply because it is live.

More resources are being allocated towards live events, live stories. In television, recorded pieces fight for smaller budgets. British drama, for example, is now produced for considerably lower sums per hour on average than in the 1990s. Great drama doesn't come cheap, and when budgets are trimmed, quality suffers. Perhaps not perceptibly at first, but erosion is invisible, until the landslide becomes apparent and it's noticed that audiences have eroded along with the quality. It's a slippery slope, and temptations of other live events, on other media, are all around. The best stories are not then necessarily found in traditional drama – they are in live events, the revived games shows, live sport.

When events are not live but attempt to ape live values, audiences know the score. Sports highlights, useful for catching up what you've missed, are considerably less dramatic – especially if the audience knows the result before tuning in. Highlights are considerably less valued to sports-adoring audiences and therefore to the sports organization selling the rights.

Live is valuable because we are more switched on than ever. If you don't know what's going on in the world as soon as it happens, or shortly after, then you're missing something. You're out of the action, unable to join in conversations. Old football scores are for anoraks. Knowing the score *now* is what counts. News is only news when it isn't old. Then it might well as be history (although there is a massive market in historical stories). When a major event happens in the world, there's not simply an expectation that people will know quickly and accurately; individuals can be at a significant loss if they're not in the know.

LIVE IS REALITY

The more connected we become, the more real-time stories we consume. Not simply real-time news and information, but more real-time real-ness. Reality stretches into our entertainment and our stories.

As we demand stories to have the appearance of live-ness and appear to be much more real, we also expect to be able to participate. News, for example, sometimes happens fast. Spectacular and unexpected events unfold before our eyes. But that's the exception. Most of the time, what we have come to term 'news' is, in fact, pre-planned 'diary' stories based around functioning of parliaments, or the courts, or local institutions, or the business calendar. It's why, in the pre-wired world, there was less news around at weekends and holidays – so much less is booked into the diary. And it's why the 24-hour, rolling-news environment has an insatiable demand for new content or new ways of refreshing old content.

> For audience participation is always a cheap, powerful way of creating content, the audience being knowledgeable amateurs who don't have to be paid for their contributions.

Interaction helps. It's a quiet news day, but you still have a newspaper to fill, a news bulletin to write, a round-the-clock news website to keep nourished with new content. In the phrase of a hit quiz show, better ask the audience.

For audience participation is always a cheap, powerful way of creating content, the audience being knowledgeable amateurs who don't have to be paid for their contributions. If the guest hasn't turned up, have a phone-in.

Online polling is one of the simplest, quickest, cheapest ways to create news and give the appearance of consultative authenticity. International polling organizations have grown fat surveying audiences' opinions; now they can be bypassed with self-selecting samples from the audience that matters – you. Think the West should launch a war against Iraq? Press red on your remote control. Should cannabis be legalized? Vote on our website. With results updated as they come in, this is speedy news creation that gathers audience data, and, when using premium-rate phone lines, can bring in a bit of cash.

It's sometimes hard to separate the real news stories from the spurious ones that have been made to order, either by the news organizations or by businesses seeking coverage. And if the audience really is on their own, in control of their own selection, how can they tell what's important and what's not? Until now, we have been used to the help of an intermediary to interpret the significance of daily news events. We call them journalists or editors.

Today's audiences no longer strictly need the intermediary, for intermediaries can get in the way of the reality. Yet the editor's role remains useful. This is the person – or team – who continues to help form community: putting a package together so that everyone can broadly agree on what are the most important issues of the day.

This philosophy, being anathema to the personalization of the digital age, is being addressed by publishers who, fearing cannibalization of their print products, have, after some initial resistance, ventured into new media.

In doing so, they have opened up part of the editing process to the audience. All the information in the world is now available on the Internet. People can personalize channels so they only receive news that is relevant to them. But crucially, unless the intermediary helps, they may miss vital information, something happening in the world, a story of importance to others around them or the wider community.

The help relies on structures and maps, a nomenclature that is clear and understood. Importance is a hierarchy – the stories that appear at the top of the news bulletin, the front page of the newspaper, or the top of the Web page in the boldest letters with the biggest graphic are the most important: stories which audiences share in order to be a community. The *Financial Times*' chief business writer Peter Martin explains:

> The nature of a newspaper is that it represents the considered view of a team of skilled people about what the most important events are over a natural and fairly substantial proportion of time – 24 hours. Readers buy that judgement as much as anything else. What the web is opening up and unbundling is that process,

allowing people to see those decisions as we go along – what is the best story at this minute, as opposed to what is the considered judgement of the day.

Opening up the process, making it more immediate, without making it available real-time, keeps some of the control with the storyteller. Audiences can see the drama unfold, but they continue to rely on the storyteller to guide them. Of course, real-time news and information are there if the audience really wants them. But if you do, you're on your own. If you have an interest in sailing, or Madonna, or exotic butterflies, technology allows you to be up to date with developments, and to share stories with your chatroom friends or bulletin board buddies throughout the world. But pick something really dull, or terribly idiosyncratic, which few others in your immediate real-world environment share, and you'll be struggling for conversation later in the bar, won't you? Community depends on shared experiences.

REAL CONVERSATIONS WITH REAL PEOPLE

So we're back in the real world trying to have a conversation. We need common stories – and they can be hard to find when there's just so much content about, and still only 24 hours in the day to find them. True personalization is struggling to emerge because, however much people say they are individuals, humans still run in packs.

Previous generations were completely unable to operate as individuals because everyone belonged to a larger social group and personal survival depended on maintaining harmony within it. Education of the masses chipped away at this dependency, starting with the concept that people were original, which developed in the Renaissance period.

Conversations happen because humans are social. Unique people feel alone. Most people don't want to spend all day, every day playing with gadgets, however useful, educational or entertaining they may be.

Conversations happen because humans have stories to share, and a common understanding of structure and nomenclature. And because conversations happen, humans tell one another which stories to look out for. People are the start of the filtering process. We are all critics who can make or break a gig.

Audiences use the filter of their peers' comments to select the good from the bad and to fit everything into their busy lives. People trust those they know more than independent critics – it's why 'viral marketing' works so well. And if they don't actually know these people, then at least they believe they are someone just like them. They do, after all, enjoy the same books and films and music. Consumers save other consumers time and money.

Research from the UK's Henley Centre for Forecasting suggests that two-thirds of people are struggling to keep up with the pace of life and have to find ways of coping. The more choices consumers have, the less time they have to choose. They want choice, they like choice, but with that choice comes greater pressure – even when selecting pleasurable things.

Even when there is time to relax, the decision about what to do is enough to raise the blood pressure. If you want to chill out with the Sunday papers, the *New York Times* regularly contains more than 300 pages. Watch television, and pick a programme from any of 200 on air right now. Only Internet directories make wading through the Web in any way a satisfying experience.

Time is such a valuable commodity that people are willing to pay for its release. Even queue-busting businesses are springing up – hand over some cash and someone with time on their hands will stand in line for you. According to the Henley Centre, more than one-third of people would pay a small fee for hired help waiting to check in for a flight (a bit of a security risk to leave your bags with strangers, but some say they are prepared to do it), 20% would pay to have someone else wait in a call-centre queue, and, amazingly, one person in 25 would pay to avoid queuing at a cashpoint – even though the whole point of a cashpoint is to avoid standing in line in the bank.

We may want to free up time to share conversations, but to do so we have to invest time having experiences and doing new things – and with the fragmentation of content into many specialist interest groups, we can find ourselves being part of a community remotely. In this respect, the technology to help us do so has come full circle. Once again, we are an audience of one.

Many people regret what they see as the breakdown of family activities: the decline of board games in favour of Game Boys, the switch from gathering round the radio to downloading music files to a mobile phone.

But there is nothing inherently collective about content consumption through the age of mass media. If you were knocking around in the 1920s, wireless meant a crystal set with lots of wires, and it was a solitary activity. It was another ten years before bigger sets became the focal points for families, very much like television of the 1960s and 1970s. Computers, like television and radio of previous generations, may reside in family rooms when first bought. That has to do with cost. As they become cheaper and smaller, they begin to infest the house.

In many households today, there are more radios than occupants. Once again radio listening is a solitary activity – particularly with personal stereos and in-car radios. With all the attention that new media technologies derive, it's easy to forget the humble radio. This, the oldest of the electronic media, reaches nine out of ten people regularly, and people listen to an average of more than 24 hours a week.

Add that to television viewing at about 27 hours a week (it had a slight dip in radio's favour in 2001), the average working week of 38 hours and sleeping at, say, 56 hours, and that leaves just 34 hours in the week to enjoy all of life's other wonders – like movies, music and the Internet. When all that's done, one still has to find the odd half-hour for family and friends. Little wonder that the personal services business – such as queue-busting – is thriving.

TURNING DRAMA INTO A GAME

Gaming is also a solitary activity, done in the privacy of one's own home. It's what teenagers get up to in their bedrooms. The vast majority of regular games players are male, and most are young. Parents hope children will grow out of the gaming bug, equating games with childhood, and if only they'd known they would never have bought the console. But the omens don't look good, and the average age of PC and console games players is creeping up – the average console buyer in 2002 was 22.6 years old according to research company IDC. UK developers estimate the average age of those playing games through interactive television was 36 in 2001. Games are addictive. Dungeons and Dragons enticed players young, who then found the addiction too strong to break. They remain hooked on character figures, board games and PC software, and many are now in their 40s or 50s.

Solitary as games experiences may often be, paradoxically they are also shared, forming communities both local and worldwide. Like cinema, games are all-consuming, with consumers fixated on a screen and mesmerized by the action played out before them. Unlike cinema and television, which are, by and large, passive experiences, gaming, particularly Internet-based interactive gaming, is a sit-up, pulsating, absorbing, sometimes white-knuckle activity.

Computer games have come from nowhere in the past ten years to be a bigger business than film or television. From the early days of Pong (which already has a place in London's Science Museum), Space Invaders and Pacman (all produced by the now-defunct Atari), successful games software regularly sells more than a million copies, more than most music album hits. The industry is worth more than $10 billion. Half of all families in the USA own a games console, and most of those that do regularly hire games. Yet this isn't a kids' business – games are rated just like movies, with many of the most desirable – if you happen to be a child – receiving 18 certificates.

If storytellers want to preview the future, they must look to interactivity and dream even bigger dreams (or nightmares, in the case of many games). A whole new generation rarely consumes much television, preferring activities that exercise their thumbs. Not all games, of course, are based around linear narrative story structures. Sports simulations, shoot-em-ups, beat-em-ups and strategy games are amongst the biggest sellers. Those not based on story may rely more on action, and all entice the player into an imaginary world.

Probably inevitably, games have spawned an academic discipline alongside film and television studies. A report by Edge presented at Games Culture 2001 in the UK termed the subject 'narratology'. The opposing school of thought is called 'ludology', deriving from the board game Ludo, which suggests that games should be treated as being distinct from any other medium and merits its own methodology. These studies at least keep academics off the streets.

Interactive games, like their childhood namesakes, involve a far deeper level of audience involvement than any other creative medium. In games, the player is the star, controlling the destiny of those around him, the other characters in the drama. Like sport, gaming is also fiercely competitive, creating another drama extraneous to the one on the screen. Gamers compete in leagues as ferocious as anything that takes place in the world's sporting arenas. It is a matter of pride and honour to rise to the top of a table, to have one's name recognized and respected among gaming peers. Games are serious stuff, not play.

Like leading characters in a film, who go through a journey and leave as changed people, games players learn through experiences. While there are many games in which chance has as much credence as skill, in others the journey is a learning experience for the character, who is, of course, the player.

A character who starts off poor and weak becomes harder, faster, stronger, bigger, richer the more the game is played. The serious gamer is a screen-based sportsman. If he wants to wipe the smile off the faces of his challengers, the game has to be played and played over again. Only with experience do characters grow. And so the games almost demand to be played.

In many fighting games, even the most useless beginner can randomly press a lot of buttons and do quite well, perhaps even becoming a grand master on a league ladder. But the bigger stories, with the potential for greatest addiction, have interactive dramatic structures, rather than being ones in which the story leads one through a narrative, predetermined path. These are the games in which a very experienced player is going to utterly tank a novice.

With Pokémon, it's impossible to beat a more experienced player. This is an addictive game that has all the characteristics of a hit property, having transferred into films, books, toys, even trainers and T-shirts (which very small children wear with pride).

Pokémon, a card and computer game that has spawned two successful films and a hit cartoon series, has an addicted following of young girls and boys who have just gotta catch 'em all. Conceived by a company called Game Freak in 1991, the trading game's target audience is under 12 years old. The game can be played with handheld devices that have to be connected together to trade. In Japan, for example, Game Boys can be connected to mobile phones and Pokémon played remotely. In the old-economy world, trading cards remain the medium favoured by children. The Pokémon franchise transcends media, old and new.

For those who haven't had the pleasure of the console game, players inhabit a bizarre world where everyone is obsessed with little creatures called Pokémons. Participants start off as a child of around eight who is desperate to become the number-one Pokémon trainer in the world. When a Pokémon is first caught, they are tiny little things, but treated well they grow big and strong. Eventually, they become fighting monsters armed with wondrous weapons.

Hairy, wizened gamers playing Pokémon for the first time will be trounced by any novice who has dabbled in the game enough to have built up even a modest pocket-monster collection. Players with serious games habits, venturing into Pokémon leagues on the Internet, ignorantly assume that their superior games-playing skills will win through. They are wrong. Their cuddly baby Diglets, the tiniest of Pokémons will never overcome Snorlax or Steelix, the game's fattest and longest characters. Try playing Pokémon as a David-and-Goliath battle, a theme upon which many myths are made, and you'll be splattered without forgiveness. Goliath takes all in Pokémon.

Good against evil is a standard among stories, and the mould from which many characters are cast – whether in films, games, fairy stories or history. If good is to prevail, then one must learn from experience, build new skills, identify strategies to overcome weakness, and work hard. If games players have addictive tendencies, these are the stories with which to ensnare them – though it is for the gamer to choose good over evil, and lots like to be baddies.

Battles, wars, action adventures, with their characters, strategies, dramas and emotions, form the basis of many interactive games, some with strong narratives, others less so. That they are popular in the digital world should come as no surprise. History is the biggest non-fiction genre for booksellers, whole television channels thrive on the subject. Every weekend on former battlefields of Europe and North America, mock regiments congregate to recreate the battles of old.

Naturally, addiction to games, to scoring points and overcoming others, whether real or not, should stay on the screen and not cross into real life. In the north of England in 2001, a 24-year-old driver mowed down an elderly pedestrian in real life, then awarded himself 100 points for killing her, boasting that it was just like Death Race 2000, in which drivers knock down people to score points. His prize: six and a half years in jail.

A ONE-WAY STREET?

While there is drama in games, not all games make great dramas. Some have made the transfer into the movies, but very few have found the magic storytelling ingredient to do so successfully. Super Mario Brothers, a massive game, proved to be a disastrous movie. Streetfighter, Wing Commander and Double Dragon have tried to make the jump to linear narrative and probably wish they hadn't.

Yet statistics are supposedly in their favour. If we're talking addiction, millions of young men who can't get enough of the action on their games consoles form a sizable core market for a filmed version. Trouble is, they just didn't trek to the movies in anywhere the same kind of numbers to give the films a substantial return. Any addiction is to playing the game, not necessarily to stories or characters. Content transfer is largely a one-way street – from other media to games, and although it can work the other way around, doing so is tough. Books can be brought to life through visual media, but interactive visual media have to have elements taken away, leading to withdrawal symptoms for addicts.

Audiences don't necessarily make the transfer as easily as the characters, because audiences want different things from different media. The expectation of a games audience is that the story is pliable, that they will follow a different path each time they play, discovering elements of the drama that many of the production team may not yet have ventured across.

Game	Film
You're the star.	The star's the star.
You control the story.	A director controls the story.
The story is different every time.	The story is the same every time.
Stories and characters can change along the way.	Stories and characters are predetermined.
Relatively inexpensive production – you, being the star, come cheap.	Big movies with big stars cost big bucks.

Games and films: story differences

Blade Runner, the game, has more than a dozen different endings, and all manner of permutations to reach one of them. But in the film, the audience is forced to accept the path that the director and writer have set, and that they believe the bulk of the audience will just love.

Loyal audiences can be trouble. In making the transfer, whatever the medium, addicted fans demand that adaptations remain true to the original. In a world of exploded content, exactly which story is the original? This appears particularly to exercise film buffs, who prefer the director's cut to theatre releases and blow gaskets at the thought of television adaptations (even if the director has made all the versions under the sun).

Blade Runner – the game again – was based around the eponymous film. In the game, players take on the role of Blade Runners hunting down rogue androids. The storyline, however, is game-specific and hardly matches the narrative of the film. Players don't get to be Harrison Ford at all, just any old Blade Runner-type agent, with a mission to kill androids and whoever else happens to get in the way (you're a policeman, so no need to bother about the law).

The point of the film is action, suspense, drama. That's the same for the game. But the game has the added attraction of being different every time, with adrenalin oozing as androids try to kill you, not Harrison Ford. That focuses the mind. The game shifts through dramatic changes of storyline, which can be played from start to finish without even coming across parts of the story. Every player has a different experience to other players, every time. That could be said of a film, just, but at least everyone shares the same journey. Games bring an added dimension.

Inside the world of computer games, there is a move away from Blade Runner-type narratives, a single-player game based around a plot, which in turn is based around a film, and towards multi-player games that have no story of their own. The only interactions are those of the players towards each another, narratives are thrown completely to the wind and it is up to the players to generate the landscape that others enter. Transferring this kind of game across to other media and creating hit properties is tremendously difficult. Profit, loyalty, addiction will have to be found within the confines of the interactive games medium.

For the creators, there is little point spending significant sums of money developing a branch of a game that few will see, however delightful they would be to aficionados. Economics, at least for now, require at least some level of narrative to keep players within certain confines of the game. This may well necessitate links within the game that bring players back to central parts of the story.

Fundamentally, new media stories are:

- *interactive* – otherwise they may as well take another form;
- *accessible* – no need to wait for someone else's schedule: the content is there whenever the audience demands it;
- *contributory* – input from players forms part of the content;
- *immersive* – consisting of highly complex virtual worlds in which players become characters;
- *deep* – there are plenty of places audiences won't see because their selected paths through the narrative don't take them there;
- *anchored* – certain key elements, whether of character, plot or action, are common to all audiences.*

Above all, the stories are multi-linear, not non-linear. They do not necessarily have strong, complete narrative – the essence of story is captured in characters, location and the unfolding nature of time – but they are recognizable as stories, in some form, nonetheless.

To transfer to other media, the story requires strength in enough key elements to match the intended medium's characteristics. So, if it is to work in film, then strong characters with clear motives following the path

---

* With thanks to Richard Fell, BBC Fictionlab, whose summary this section is built on.

along a narrative structure work best. It may make a television series if characters are strong even though there is no one single story. They then enjoy episodic interactions week by week. The story can express itself one way on the Web, another in weekly drama, another on film. No individual audience member needs to participate in all parts of the story – each bit is enjoyable enough in itself. But if it truly captures the imagination – turning into a hit property – audiences transfer to follow the content, and the whole is bigger than the sum of the parts.

But these are early days. Few producers have really explored the potential for drama on the Internet. Entertainment, news and music have all transferred much better. Film-makers may be using interactive tools to promote productions, but hardly any have developed the motivations of their characters on the Web, or built their back story – their history – so that audiences have a new understanding of the characters' actions on screen.

All that is to come.

There's something about those irritating people who always seem to know the ending of a story before everyone else. The kind of people who say, 'He did it, I've seen it before,' during a murder mystery, or who talk loudly about the ending of a film as they pass the queue on its way into the cinema. These are the people who have got one over on everyone else. They're first. Everyone else follows. If you want to beat these people, you need to keep up with a story that goes on 24 hours a day.

Big Brother, global television phenomenon, creates stories from the mundane and manages to produce enough material, across many media, for anyone who cares to watch all day, every day. With new content – sometimes not very interesting content – only the most addicted viewers can keep up with subtext and plot for every character. Yet with real-time video on the Web and on digital television, viewers can be up to speed with events and obscure facts well ahead of their friends who watch only packaged highlights. *Big Brother* is a self-perpetuating publicity machine. It transfers.

A voyeuristic fantasy?

Here's the scenario. A group of young men and women locked in a house, totally cut off from the outside world. Food and booze are rationed, though treats can be earned for self-ridicule beyond a normal sense of duty, and contestants undergo constant scrutiny by videocamera – even as they sleep. Each must carry a personal microphone, and each must nominate a fellow contestant once a week for eviction. It's a game for which there is a big cash prize – about three times average annual earnings in the UK – unlimited publicity, and free post-series psychiatric counselling. Viewers can follow multiple plotlines by selecting which camera to follow on digital television, while the Web provides the opportunity to comment and discover more about the characters. In addition to sales of the programme, incremental income is generated by text message to mobile devices, through premium-rate phone calls to vote on eviction, and paraphernalia such as book tie-ins and videos.

The global franchise

George Orwell may have coined the phrase in *Nineteen Eighty-four*, but much of the western world today equates Big Brother with a flirting and gossipy television show. Dutch production company Endemol created and licenses *Big Brother*, which first aired in The Netherlands in 1999.

The content quickly became a global franchise, extending across media, adapted to local markets. Wherever in the world one switches to *Big Brother*, it is instantly recognizable, though characters and language may be alien. It is always live, or nearly live, with immediacy creating drama. The more the show is talked about, the greater the revenues as audiences interact.

The French version of *Big Brother*, *Loft Story*, propelled broadcaster M6 to market leadership in its slot, attracting a 40 per cent TV audience share. In the USA, the website of *Big Brother* broadcaster CBS achieved its highest ever traffic figures, with 34 million page views and half a million log-ins to *Big Brother* chat. In both the UK and Australia, *Big Brother* websites crashed under the strain. However, other than RTL.de, the German broadcaster's website, which increased its reach by three percentage points during transmission, no European television channel has been able to sustain onsite audience growth following the peak audience which Big Brother brought (Jupiter Media Metrix, 2002).

Big Brother created material for other media, with the backstories of contestants providing editorial content for other broadcasters and newspapers. Each series has a unit of press officers to generate coverage. The media frenzy is self-fulfilling, with press stories bringing in new audiences, or encouraging viewers to return – which in turn increases the interest in press coverage. During the first series run in the UK, popular newspaper sales rose when *Big Brother* stories appeared on the front page. The *Mirror* reported one of its highest Friday sales in several years when it ran a front-page photograph of three female *Big Brother* residents naked in the tub.

A lot of sticky content

Live, lengthy content that creates characters and tells a story is attractive material. Relatively inexpensive to produce in terms of cost per hour, it's malleable material that can be edited into short segments, streamed from multiple cameras, and summarized as text. *Big Brother* is a big story, launched in the accessible arena of national television, which transfers to other media.

In the UK, *Big Brother* formed the spine of terrestrial broadcaster Channel 4's new youth channel E4, which ran the programme live (with a short time delay to prevent the transmission of inappropriate material) 18 hours a day – including those not very interesting hours when the house-mates slept. On an interactive platform, audiences could time-shift, access news summaries, and choose camera angles. E4's digital television audience share rose fourfold during *Big Brother* weeks.

Cross-promotion encourages audiences to sample the story in different media. Live material for many weeks on the Web and interactive television doesn't necessarily create addictive content of itself. With so many characters in an unscripted environment, the story is pretty hard to follow. It needs an intermediary, an editor, to package the material. This forms the central daily highlights show. Drama is created by challenges set by the producers, by the weekly eviction, and by the relationships that develop between the participants.

Producer Conrad Green attributes *Big Brother*'s success to three points of tension and control. It is a show in which the producer can intervene only at a certain point; where the people in the house can determine their fate only to a certain point; and in which the audience can control the story, but not completely (Wells, 2001).

In addition to sales of programme rights, *Big Brother* is a multimedia money spinner – but the old-fashioned telephone is the most profitable way of generating incremental income. For the first eviction of the UK series, 400,000 people voted using premium-rate phone lines costing 25 pence a time. Over the seven-week series, that's an income of £700,000 – quite a tidy sum with which to supplement the show's main income. In France, Jupiter MMXI estimates that more than five million euros were spent on text messages during a *Big Brother* series. Although advertising has surrounded website content, in a similar way to advertising being contained within television programme breaks, *Big Brother* Internet sites have generated only marginal revenues for paid-for content. Most successful was the US *Big Brother* association with RealNetworks (now RealOne), where more than 50,000 users paid $20 for a season's worth of online video.

Big Brother customized content to each medium. The main television programme is a narrative format, placing events of the past 24 hours into story format, presenting highlights and anecdotes, and summarizing the state of play. The website is a place to keep up with live events through the day, when the audience could not access television. Viewers could also join in discussions, vote, bet and play games. Streamed content is on the Web and interactive television. Text messages are sent to mobile phones. And there's a book of the show, plenty of lively copy in the papers, and a *Big Brother* board game. The story transfers.

REFERENCES

Jupiter Media Metrix, Long-term effect of Big Brother on interactivity, February 2002.

Matt Wells, 'There's no such thing as reality TV', the *Guardian*, 5 November 2001.

FINDING THE AUDIENCE

5

'All the world's a stage
    And all the men and women merely players.'

William Shakespeare

Creative businesses are built on developing content and delivering it to audiences. What the audience likes, the audience gets in spades. But finding what audiences like is elusive. Discover this magic and the better the prospect of keeping people coming back for more.

Yet it is so difficult to find a handful of people who can actually agree on what an audience looks like in the first place. Even long-established media share no universal recognition about what an audience actually is. Most other businesses are crystal clear about those with whom they communicate and upon whom they rely to survive – they are customers. But media businesses and the creative types within them are rarely comfortable thinking about themselves as businesses at all.

So instead of customers, they have listeners, or viewers, or 'goers' – as in movie-goers or theatre-goers. Sometimes, audiences are 'punters'. Digital media exacerbates already problematic semantics. Here, the audience is not an audience at all, say digital gurus, because digital delivery, especially with interactive content, creates individual stories. It's one to one. By definition, one person isn't a collective, and audiences, surely, are collectives. There's nothing collective about sitting alone in an office or bedroom joining in with a story in which you, the user (the audience), can dictate the narrative.

So digital content creators avoid the word 'audience'. Instead, they have 'users', a drug analogy suggesting addiction. 'Viewers' is too reminiscent of old-economy TV, which new media simply isn't meant to ape. 'Viewers' isn't a term with widespread new-media usage, despite the fact that page views are a key measure of success for websites and the currency with which many sell content to advertisers or sponsors. Page views, presumably, aren't read by page viewers. These people are 'eyeballs'.

Digital broadcaster Music Choice is one new-media company that sometimes struggles to find the right word with which to define its audience. Being delivered on digital devices to the home, people generally consume the service individually or in small groups. Here is a new service with a strong proposition – it broadcasts more than 40 channels of non-stop music, no DJs, videos or commercial breaks, on television, on the Internet, and on new mobile devices. Are its customers listeners (it broadcasts music), viewers (it comes on television), subscribers (they have to pay the distributor every month) or users (they can check out what music is playing and, soon, buy it)? Transferring across media can make you schizophrenic.

On the whole, the word 'audience' just doesn't seem to work for new media, say many content producers. 'Audience' is old economy. Audiences are bulk commodities, and somewhat dated.

If that's the case, why not stick with 'customers'? Why insist on terms of avoidance like 'users'? Customers, it appears, is just too damned commercial as a concept for producers, with a whiff of a suggestion that someone might have to go and sell them something. It's a lament of many creatives, particularly when fighting finance and marketing people, that their products are regarded as products at all. 'We're not selling cans of beans,' they complain. But they are fighting for customers in a competitive marketplace, where audiences assert their power as consumers, choosing what to hear, see and read from a much wider spectrum. Producers better get organized. A common language and an understanding of the fragmented audience – how people consume content both as a collective and as individuals – is a start.

There's an old, not particularly useful saying, that if something looks like an elephant, walks like an elephant, and smells like an elephant, then it is probably an elephant. If these people, who, whether they come together in one place, or sit in a darkened room and rarely leave the house by day, patronize your product in a way that causes you to make a bit of money or add brightness into their lives, then collectively this is an audience. Taken singularly, they are customers. There is no shame in deciding audience are customers, but there has been resistance to the concept, borne out of limited supply of content by a privileged few to what should be the grateful many.

THE OLD CHOICE IS NO CHOICE

Life used to be easy, fun and well paid for those working in storytelling media. With fewer outlets, it may have been harder to get a job, but once you were in, the chances were strong that you were in for life. And if your story had the good fortune to be produced (not all were – it was a perk of the job that one could be hired as a journalist or producer and sit around in bars for years waiting for an idea to ferment), its chance of being seen or heard was relatively high.

There simply used to be so much less content knocking about from which audiences could choose. A generation ago, three network television stations served the USA. Three channels broadcast in the UK. Much of continental Europe was similarly scant, for spectrum was scarce and regulated strongly. Cinema multiplexes had yet to be thought of. Magazines and newspapers, costly enough to produce, were difficult to store and ship, so titles were limited.

But if you did build content, chances were quite high that audiences would come. The audience of old was brought together by compulsion – choice was more than limited. In some cases – UK broadcasting, or US local newspapers – there was no choice at all. One size had to fit all.

Anyone listening to radio in the UK not so long ago faced a very simple choice – the BBC or, after dark and with sound quality that today would have them closed down through a dearth of listeners (which, in the end, is exactly what happened), Radio Luxembourg. On the BBC, Radio 1 bizarrely became Radio 2 after 7.30 in the evening (and originally in the daytime too), as did local radio. No matter how many times you twiddled the dial, *Sing Something Simple* was the liveliest music to be had. On station after station after station.

Lack of choice does bring one major advantage to producers whatever business they're in. More customers. They may be a bit disgruntled, or they may be thankful for having any kind of service at all. But they do form a sizable collective. And because there's not much else around to entertain them, they do come back. This is the old form of audience loyalty – people turning to the same content out of habit rather than delight. Choosing the same newspaper because it's the best of a bad lot. Watching the same television channel because 'we always do'.

Sunday evenings on television used to mean religion, like it or not, because that's what the regulators insisted was in the public interest. People watched. And, like eager delegates at a convents' convention, thousands of people got into the habit. In 2001, Australian soap opera *Home and Away* switched channels from market-leading ITV, where it achieved an audience of more than five million, to market-laggard Channel 5. The hit show, addictive viewing for teenagers and elderly daytime television viewers, appeared to lose three million viewers in the transfer. All these people had to do was flick a different button on the remote control. Sometimes, it isn't the content that's addictive. It's the habit of going somewhere. The total television audience at that time scarcely changed. Viewers stuck to the channels they were used to.

Identify an audience's consumption habits and you're half way there to getting them to sample content. If you can create material that replaces content in the same slot or medium where a large audience already exists – or somewhere around it – many people will try it out. Just out of habit. Just because they come to that place at that time, whether it's a website, newspaper, music store or cinema. After all, addiction is only habit with heightened severity. We've all seen plenty of bad films because we sometimes go to the cinema or watch late-night television regardless of what's showing. Building or placing content that exploits existing habits is sensible business.

THE FEW INTO THE MANY

Paucity of choice once led to a self-perpetuating community of people who saw the same films, heard the same songs, read the same books. If you were around in the 1940s and lived in the USA, you could pop into a bar and talk about the latest events in *Dragnet* and just about everyone would know what you were talking about. The show was NBC Radio's hit weekly drama, and with few other networked serials around, and not much other radio at all, it soon gained a following of loyal listeners. When *Dragnet* transferred to television in 1952, it and its star Jack Webb brought along an addicted audience. Like all good stories, the show spawned great catchphrases – 'The story you have just seen is true. The names were changed to protect the innocent'. If you recognize that, it's not only to do with the power of *Dragnet* as a 1950s television and radio programme. It's about powerful storytelling, passed down through generations by word of mouth.

In the UK, people talk in revered tones about *The Goons* and *That was the Week that Was*. Great shows, maybe, but shows that nonetheless had to fight a little less hard for a share of the audience than they would have done today. Both have endured, certainly in the hearts of their original audiences. But they have transferred too, being available to new consumers through books and audio cassettes, and even young customers can enjoy the old humour (www.goons-online.co.uk, for example, is a fan website written by a university student).

Dragnet: started on radio, transferred to television.
Source: Getty Images/Hulton Archive

As the sheer volume of content available has increased, so has the belief that audience loyalty can be won by crafting whole channels that match niche preferences more precisely. Into sport, here's a sports channel. Not targeted enough? Have a soccer station. Still not satisfied? How about something dedicated to your own particular club? Already, there's bags of digital content around specific sports stars, with agents tying up deals with content providers to tell more of their stars' stories. So, for an update of how the midfielder feels training went this morning, he'll text you from the dressing-room … when you subscribe, of course.

At the start of the transition between very few channels and the very many, the theory was that segmentation would lead to loyal audiences almost by default. The closer one is to matching audience preference, the stronger the bond the audience feels towards the channel.

But now there are hundreds of very, very niche channels, segmentation has given way to fragmentation. Segments are chunky – no longer the amorphous mass, an audience lumped together and whose main value is in its size. Segments have value that grows the total value cake because segmentation is a currency for marketers who buy the audience in bits, paying premiums for some. That makes it an attractive concept for producers too – though it may be a bit ambitious to believe that people who can't bring themselves to use words like 'audience' or 'customer' will ever get their tongues round the 's' word.

> **The result of fragmentation is that finding audiences sizable enough to provide robust and regular sources of income is tough.**

Fragments, by contrast, are not that great. These are the splinters, the things left lying around when the juicier segments have been swept up. The result of fragmentation is that finding audiences sizable enough to provide robust and regular sources of income is tough. Too often, niche hasn't equated to well-targeted. It has just meant small.

If broadcasters, film producers and publishers find fragmentation hard, then free-standing Web players face an almost impossible task in attracting large audiences and finding ways of making them profitable. Advertisers will pay for some niche audiences if the niche is attractive and if the costs of reaching this kind of audience make the effort worthwhile. Some niche audiences will pay for content from their own pockets providing the content is good enough (sports and music are most notable examples again, although so is pornography). On the whole, though, to reach audiences sizable enough to make content production worthwhile, it helps to be big and to tell your story in many media.

THE HETEROGENEOUS AUDIENCE

Not only does the audience now have much more content to choose from; they also have many more devices available with which to access that content. Everyone has a radio, just about everybody has a television and telephone (many people, of course, have more than one of each), and we're getting to the stage, despite the fear of an information-poor under-class, where everyone has access to a computer should they want it, to the Internet, and to any number of other gizmos and gadgets.

The combination of more content and more devices makes delivering great stories to loyal audiences tremendously complex. With so many possible permutations, the audience is no longer homogeneous.

That's not to say the audience as a collective has ceased to exist. Creative storytellers can devise many scenarios for the audience to follow, but they can rarely create an individual story for an individual audience member. The audience must take control for themselves in order to do that.

The more markets fragment, the more that audiences for any particular shred, on average, go down. Increasingly, today's audience is fragmented, not segmented, just like the channels. This is what digital has done. A fragmented audience splits its loyalty between many choices and is then less loyal to that choice. (According to Professor Patrick Barwise of London Business School, this is double jeopardy, also seen with branded goods.) There's so much to choose from that you can be as disloyal as you like, for the bonds of community are weaker. Fragmentation begets infidelity.

Despite fragmentation, audience behaviour and preferences have not fundamentally changed. Total television viewing, for example, has been pretty steady over the years, even as new forms of entertainment have intruded. An alien arriving on the planet to study television viewing patterns in the western world (doesn't sound like the greatest blockbuster, does it?) could look at the ratings and not figure out that the Internet had arrived. There have been changes to individual programme and channel ratings, and audiences fragment, but weekly viewing hours remain high.

As audiences to individual pieces of content get smaller, it becomes ever more important to create addictive content that transfers across media, attracting new audiences along the way and bringing a loyal following to each medium. Content becomes a hit property, not just a hit – a franchise that has value. In the USA, public service broadcaster PBS has long been the minority TV channel, eschewing high-rating comedies, quizzes and dramas in favour of programming that may not otherwise be aired in the commercially cut-throat environment of US television. Audiences, although relatively small, exhibit fierce loyalty to both the programming and the concept of public service broadcasting. Former PBS director John Hollar, now head of Pearson Broadband, explains:

People feel stronger about PBS and want to know more. This creates a huge momentum to provide something once the programmes are over, and we fastened on quickly to the notion that the internet was somewhere people could go to get information. We called it the 'TV plus internet' strategy. So, for example, when you finish watching a documentary about Winston Churchill on TV, on the internet there is a vast repository of background information, production notes, video clips and so on to view at your own pace. PBS increased the amount of time audiences spent with the content and not, as other broadcasters feared, avoided the internet because they were afraid it would somehow cannibalise their broadcast efforts.

Split the population into narrower demographics and the change in consumption of both content and media become apparent. Among teenagers in particular, television viewing is down, although teens have always spurned the box for other habits of their age. Young people are the biggest players of games consoles, with many children expressing a preference for the interaction of games over the relative passivity of television. They also enjoy a higher disposable income than past generations, which they need if they are to indulge in the latest shoot-em-up software.

Heterogeneity in content consumption, borne of a multiplicity of devices and a flood of new content, makes defining audiences all the more tricky. Are games players who simultaneously listen to music games players, music listeners, or both? Is someone who watches television while reading the paper a viewer or a reader at that moment in time? What if the set is on but no one is really paying attention? Is it a soundtrack being consumed in a different way from that which the producer intended? Leisure multi-tasking means that, cumulatively, many people could consume more content than a 24-hour day logically allows.

This is the age of continuous partial attention. Only in the cinema or theatre, when the lights go down, do we concentrate on the story unfolding before our eyes (while eating popcorn, balancing drinks, fiddling with the programme, and perhaps having a snog). The heterogeneous audience is an audience for many things all at the same time.

This makes predicting consumption patterns somewhat difficult. Being available to consume something doesn't necessarily mean audiences *will* consume. Being in the market to buy something doesn't mean the audience won't be tempted just to borrow it from someone else if they can, or even download it for free. Often, audiences need the permission of others before they consume content. A group has to reach consensus before choosing what film to see, or a child may need authorization from a parent before cash is released for a piece of games software, or for a previously barred area of the Internet to be unlocked.

In 2001, the UK's main commercial television channel ITV paid an awful lot of money for Premiership soccer rights, announcing they were to change what people watched on Saturday nights. Sport supplanted programming aimed largely at women as the anchor of the early-evening schedule. But football's core audience – men – whom advertisers crave, simply don't have permission to watch television, and particularly not football, at 7 p.m. on Saturdays, so the show bombed. Men who are football fans may well have been out watching a game in the afternoon, or due to play the following morning, or they may spend a considerable amount of time talking about it to their mates. A universal truth is that when men talk about football, women extract a price. That price is a wholehearted contribution to the household on Saturday evenings – by way of putting children to bed, fixing dinner, cleaning up. They are *available* to participate, but actually taking part just isn't allowed – unless it's through a non-intrusive medium (so score updates to mobile phones, or audio content that can be consumed while the audience gets on with other things will work better). Football isn't an isolated example. If you are to find the audience, you have to consider social interactions that affect their ability to consume.

This heterogeneous audience isn't prepared to be bounced around by the schedules of others. Consumers are now too used to playing by their own rules. That makes it much harder to predict what the new heterogeneous audience wants? New research is called for.

RESEARCH OF THE IMAGINATION

Measurement data are becoming easier to come by and harder to understand, particularly given the uncertainties about what is a consumer and what isn't. Even trends through the years now no longer seem to compare like with like. Is success the amount of time people spend with the medium? 1010 Win news radio in New York for example, in common with many news stations, prides itself on giving listeners the world in 20 minutes. Audiences use the station to hear what they need and then get out again, and for that they come back.

Almost everything digital can be measured precisely – the number of viewers to this, the number of recipients of that. But for an industry that can't even agree on a term for the customer, common standards of measurement still seem some way off.

Qualitatively, there is significant resistance to measuring the effectiveness of content itself. It's little use creating the most compelling story, of the highest quality, if it's not delivered in the right way or if audiences don't feel as excited as the producers. Artists want their stories heard, but sometimes they're a little bit sensitive about the audience having too much influence. Researching their needs can be a touchy subject.

In business, research is the tool by which one decides whether to take the risk. It's a logical, scientific process. Present a certain number of people with a concept and, on the basis of the response, predict whether sufficient sales will result from the investment.

It's harder in music, or films, or games. How do audiences know what they like until they've heard or seen it? Before launching long-running serial drama *Eastenders*, the BBC tested the concept in a telephone survey. Just 13 per cent of respondents said they would be very interested in the idea. The series has now aired for the best part of 20 years and is the broadcaster's highest-rated programme, a staple of its main TV channel four nights a week. Yet an early analyst said (Buckingham, 1987):

> Audience research appears to have been used largely as a means of confirming beliefs which were already held, and as valuable ammunition in arguing the case with senior management … where research came up with information which contradicted those beliefs, it was ignored.

With larger sums of money risked to create blockbuster hits, minimizing the downside is crucial. While producers, particularly writers, work in isolation, crafting what they hope will become masterpieces, before productions go too far, there's a growing tendency to anticipate audience demand rather than launching into projects with the hope that everything will turn out all right in the end.

That sounds like reasonable business judgement. Few people would want to risk time and money creating something no one wants to buy. But the most powerful creative content is characterized by the strength of an idea, and ideas and imagination can't be measured or researched easily. How does the audience know what it likes until it has seen it?

IS ANYBODY LISTENING?

Exactly who should listen to the audience? The producer of the content, the marketing people who claim to be the consumers' champion, the distributors who are so vital to getting the product into the hands of customers, or sales people who have to make the whole thing pay its way?

UK television hit drama producer Andy Harries fights this battle, and fears that audiences will find it ever harder to locate stories that will bind them together.

> I had a big row about comedy drama *Cold Feet* [which became a hugely successful series]. I said it should go out at nine o'clock on Sunday night, and the ad sales guy was saying it should be on at ten. My argument as the producer was that it was a broad show and I felt it could be a big show with big volume. His argument was that he didn't need the extra audience and that people wanted things like *London's Burning* [a known success, which had been running in that slot for about ten years] because, he said, *London's Burning* is an ironing show. At nine o'clock people were doing the ironing and are only half watching the telly, and don't want anything to be too clever or too complicated. I think that underestimates the audience, and it's a constant problem in the television industry.

Just how carefully should one listen to the audience? Listen too much, and the world becomes formulaic – audiences can only express ideas in terms of what they have come across before, and to which they can do the ironing, or any of hundreds of other activities in this world of continuous partial attention. Listen too little, and risk self-indulgent creations that speak to too few.

In researching audience trends for music, the more popular or memorable a track is, the more likely it is to come to mind. For those planning radio schedules, if audience research isn't ignored in favour of instinct, then the station can end up reflecting the soundtrack of a wedding party reception. You know the kind of thing – 'Hi Ho Silver Lining', followed by an unfortunate revival of Boney M tracks, before Status Quo rock all over the world. One gets stuck with old standards when listening to the most vocal among the audience – the fanatics, the people with the longest memories. Each medium has its own breed of fanatic – the Star Wars fans, the Dr Who fans, the Elvis Presley fans. Listening to the coolest people can be just as devastating, producing a mix of obscure new material that is some time away from becoming mainstream. Creative art is hard work – you have to know when to listen to audiences and when to ignore them.

Content is like any new product. It goes through a product lifecycle, where public perception is pretty low at the start and pretty high at the end. But perception and sales are not the same thing at all.

In terms of their preference for new songs, for example, audiences simply rate new releases as neutral – not having heard it, they're neither for nor against. In radio stations, a creative decision about playing new material is required, for the audience can't be relied upon to pass judgement about something they don't know. As the song's lifecycle matures, one has to balance which bits of research to rely on – the market share figures (in the case of music, represented by the singles charts) or subjective preferences of the audience.

UK radio group GWR director Simon Cooper explains:

> In the early stages [of a hit record lifecycle], audiences get really excited about a record because it is new and fresh and they like listening to it, so we would play it a lot at that stage. In our research, which we do four nights a week, we ask: 'Would you rate the song as a favourite, or do you like it, are you undecided, or don't you like it?' The final question is 'Are you getting fed up with it?'

That is the point at which the audience's listening preference conflicts with market share figures. Here are people stating that they're bored with content, and yet the market appears to be lapping it up.

In 1991 Bryan Adams, topped the charts with *'Everything I Do I Do it for You'*, the theme of hit movie *Robin Hood Prince of Thieves*. In the UK, the song was number one in the charts for 16 weeks. A radio station taking its playlist from the charts would have played that song relentlessly for many months – and many did, driving many listeners to distraction (or at least to other radio stations, or their CD collections). GWR spotted the burnout, the 'fed-up' option, at a point when Adams' reign at the top still had many weeks to go. Audiences continue to buy, but do not necessarily like listening to the song over and over again on the radio, because 'buying to keep' and the desire to hear right now are not necessarily linked.

In the Bryan Adams case, many record-buyers bought the disc as a memento to the film, bringing chart longevity and annoying the pants off anyone else trying to get to number one.

The art in creating new material is knowing when not to listen to customers, having a willingness to separate oneself from what people are talking about today in order to give them what they will be talking about tomorrow.

LISTEN TO THE AUDIENCE ONLY IF IT PAYS

An audience – your customers – are just the people who listen to your story. It could be 50 million people, it could just be one. Clearly, the most successful storytellers tell their story to the widest possible audience, and make some money out of it. Instinct and methodology create a potent combination.

A clinical methodology for finding the maximum possible audience concerns, just as it does in business, customer acquisition and retention. Addiction is about getting people hooked and then making sure they stay hooked. Once addicted, storytellers can do pretty much what they like to the audience and they'll stick around. And if acquisition costs are cheap, then even if audiences withdraw or die – just as addicts do – they can be replaced quickly.

Addiction is about getting people hooked and then making sure they stay hooked. Once addicted, storytellers can do pretty much what they like to the audience and they'll stick around.

Take, for example, the newspaper business. The cost of acquiring a customer is remarkably cheap. Papers are pumped out through a distribution system and land near to the audience's homes first thing every morning. Obtaining new customers should be relatively easy – if only they weren't so addicted to some other title.

On the positive side, tempting new readers with screaming headlines, exclusive photos and tantilizing offers can cause a switch of allegiance, or an additional, temporary purchase. This is where creativity thrives and new audiences may be found.

Correspondingly, on the negative side, it's tempting to treat audiences with indifference when replacing them is cheap. Storytellers are in charge when acquisition costs are low. If it's proving too costly to provide a specialist service in a newspaper – a new way of calculating racing odds, perhaps – even though the readership loves it, it can be dropped without too much fuss. Readers who complain can easily be ignored or brushed off. There's a danger that a competitor will snap up the racing tips franchise, but so what if the cost-benefit analysis shows it to be not profitable? New readers can be attracted to something else, something cheaper. A new columnist, a fresh spin on the horoscopes, a brilliant sales promotion.

Economically, there's a point at which audiences just aren't worth listening to. Customer service can go to hell. Creative decisions are made by creatives, not by customers.

That's at odds with just about every management text under the super soar-away sun. Truly customer-responsive businesses pride themselves on listening to customers, or at least pride themselves on saying they do. Creative businesses, by contrast, are honest businesses. They want big audiences, but only big audiences who want what they've got to sell. Listening to customers? How quaint, they would seem to be saying, or even, of old, how dangerous.

John Reith, the famous, fabled founder of the BBC, actually feared that taking the pulse of what his customers wanted (he would never have thought of them as customers, of course) would be more than detrimental to the business (another term to be avoided). It would be a very bad thing indeed. Reith believed that consulting with the audience 'would inevitably influence and even dictate broadcasting policy, that worthwhile minority programmes would be sacrificed to popularity ratings' (Crissell, 1994). Reith lost the battle and a research department was established in 1936. He resigned two years later.

Reith appeared contemptuous of the vast majority of his audience. Leading a great cultural organization from the front, he knew what was best for the masses.

If his approach seems patriarchal today, Reith's concept of audience research (lack of) was not uncommon. But some producers tried.

When, in 1942, RKO Pictures previewed Orson Welles' *The Magnificent Ambersons* to audiences before its release in the general market, the omens were far from good. So completion of the film was taken away from Welles, new scenes were added, and a much-maligned happy ending scripted by an anonymous staff writer was inserted at the behest of the studio. Welles had already reduced the original length of the film by 17 minutes by the time his replacement hacked another 50 minutes off it, leaving him to complain that the heart of his picture had been destroyed. But in its new form, it won an Academy Award nomination and is remembered as the director's most important film after *Citizen Kane*, proving that authors don't always understand the impact of their work without testing it.

Today, Hollywood studios churn out more than one film a day, and a typical movie gets nine previews before release. The ones that do make it to the screen have been tested repeatedly along the way – first by creative professionals, then by studio executives who green-light projects, and ultimately in preview theatres. Audience response results occasionally lead to tensions between producers and financiers, the former understandably reluctant to change their work, the latter to make as many people happy as possible.

It's commercially important to do so when costs are high. It can cost a billion dollars to produce and market a major film. In the USA, box-office profit can only be reached if American movie-goers convince others to see the film, or go back themselves more than once. And real money is only forthcoming from ancillary sales – video rentals, sales, syndication to broadcasters and, if a real sticky story has been found, merchandising and digital content with a revenue stream.

But research that causes the story to change should ring alarm bells. If the strongest stories come from imagination, and are well told, then changing them usually means the work hasn't been thorough enough before testing, or the concept is weak. Research plays a more positive role when it provides direction for marketing. If more men than women like the product, or more young people than old people like it, then that information can be acted upon.

THE NUMBERS

One major difference between old media and new is the possibility of very precise audience-measurement criteria. Businesses that charge for sending text messages, for example, know exactly how many are being sent (although that still doesn't always equate to them being received, opened and read).

Data permit decision-making based on reality, not guesswork and instinct. Intangible services are troublesome to measure, but even imprecise research can protect services from the chop. If you can't really say how large one's audience is, well, it just could be large. Or important. Television audiences, measured by Barb in the UK and Neilson in the USA, both of whom use statistically representative samples to calculate audience size. Each audience panel results in a more or less accurate reflection of the audience, forming the currency by which advertisements are sold and programmes stay on the schedule.

Yet the stated audience size contains a sampling error of about three per cent higher or lower. It's easy to forget sampling error, believing the published audience size – one simple figure measured in millions – to be absolute fact. Only intangible services suffer in this way. It can't happen, of course, with sales of records, where a physical product, a CD, still goes out of the door, or with cinema admissions, where one human body physically passes another, handing over a stub of a ticket (technology has been slow coming to movie theatres). These audience figures are generally accurate down to the last unit. However, intangible services measured with a three per cent sampling error mean that something achieving a reputed audience of, say, ten million, and beating another achieving nine and a half million, could actually be getting the same rating. The wrong show could be hailed a success, the other confined to one-hit hell. Intangible audiences exist in isolation, often in the audience's own homes, and form only a semblance of reality, if at all, in statistical league tables.

But these tables are important, for reputation, creative pride, business success. They are the creative expression of market share – who is beating who, and in which markets. It's a fast-moving, and very public expression of share, which everyone wants to win. To inflate the numbers, manipulation is manifest and masquerades as marketing. Newspapers have bulk sales – batches bought by airlines and hotels and given away as freebies. The print equivalent of the free shower cap.

Twenty years ago in the record business, a song going straight to the top of the charts in its first week of release was a rarity. Today, it's often an expectation of record companies, so sufficient demand must be created rather than left to scheduling chance or, heaven forbid, the quality of the music. Most singles are made available to broadcasters weeks ahead of their availability in the shops, building up a raging demand among anxious fans (or perhaps seething disappointment if the content is not up to scratch). The intention is that the song should debut at the chart pinnacle. Now, although debuts at number one are routine, singles do not necessarily sell as well as in previous generations. Once again, there's so much more content available and new ways of consuming. Sales may mislead about actual consumption. Not everyone will have paid.

What is now called peer-to-peer (record companies have referred to it as stealing) isn't new. Only the technologies are, bringing the ability to swap content in seconds. With the audience in greater control of availability and scheduling distributors wisely try to show willing, being seen to be as customer-friendly as possible. It's an unenviable business balance, which affects margins (being a more competitive, oversupplied environment, pressures on price are strong). So, in record shops, listening posts are almost standard, where you can try before you buy. Selected tracks are released, sometimes in full, often in part, on the Internet. Previously, consumers would have had to take a risk and buy the whole album. Now stores may offer a 28-day return policy – just bring it back if you don't like it. An open invitation to burn your own CD and return it. But if wine shops can do it, and it builds consumer loyalty, one may as well take the risk, as piracy is a reality anyway. Most reasonable people are reasonably willing to pay reasonable amounts for quality content, if it is packaged creatively.

That big numbers are harder to achieve in the new-media era is not simply a matter of segmentation or technological advancement. It is also to do with audience availability. People consume content when they are able (and willing) to consume it, and not otherwise. Sounds obvious? The numbers may mask reality. A television show that appears to gain a regular audience figure, which varies little from programme to programme, may look like it has the same people absolutely hooked, come what may. There may well be a sizable core who do happen to see every single programme. But many others watch because they are at home and available to watch. When they're out, they don't. Only a small percentage set the video, and of those that do, not everyone gets round to playing back the tape (or, worse, has managed to actually record the right thing).

Until the invention of the video recorder, and even for a time afterwards, the television premier of a feature film was a big thing in the schedules, and for the audience. People would look forward to the main movie on a Sunday evening, or wait in eager anticipation of what cinematic treat broadcasters would be serving up on Christmas Day.

Life has changed. Films are no longer events because there are just so many opportunities to see the story any time. Previously, if you missed a movie when it first came to theatres, your chance was gone for three or four years until it popped up on television. 'Popped up' is the wrong phrase. 'Built up' into a major highlight of the week or even season would be more accurate.

That era is gone, and broadcasters now have to create other events for their schedules. Schedules no longer achieve the ratings they once did as audiences choose when to consume. Music companies no longer exclusively dictate in which order tracks go – we download tracks and cut our own discs. Audiences, not distributors, are in control.

THE AUDIENCE TAKES CONTROL

'So much time, so little to do. Scratch that. So little time, so much to do.'

Willy Wonka, living as he did in Roald Dahl's chocolate factory, with every high-tech gadget he could dream up, still suffered the stresses of work and life balance. And he's a fictional character.

Many in the audience rarely find enough time to enjoy being a passive consumer, absorbing all the content put before them. Given choice, consumers take it, but they have to make active decisions if they are to select the content that is most satisfying for them.

Critics have found their services in ever greater demand as audiences suffer from scarcity of time. Critics supply content that comments on other content – in turn, increasing the sheer volume of content in the market. And so, the audience has to make another judgement – exactly which critics should they trust?

Criticism, reviews, endorsements, advertisements – the audience has to sift and select. The first source for trusted advice tends to be friends and family. Between 50 and 70 per cent of purchases are made following the advice of friends, rather than the temptations of advertising or the reliance on one's own judgement. This is the power of word of mouth. And negative word of mouth travels between three and five times faster than positive (Horovitch and Panak, 1992). It's why producers, indeed any manufacturer, should spend more time wooing and reassuring existing customers. Attracting new customers requires audiences to give up more precious time trying the unknown. The odds are just so much longer.

Audiences have to decide what to read, see and hear. Despite the rise of continuous partial attention, in which they consume content more than ever, often at the same time, they just can't do it all. Among the decisions they have to make, customers must choose:

- how much time to devote to each medium;
- the attention they give to it;
- whether consumption will be a solitary activity or take place in a group;
- where and how it will be consumed;
- whether to indulge in a passive or interactive experience;
- what, if anything, to pay for the pleasure.

Some of these choices are relatively new, and audiences are still finding their feet, unsure how to play the new game that has transferred powers to them. It is a change from content being pushed out to grateful recipients, and their choices affect the business of producing and distributing content.

The BBC's director of new media, Ashley Highfield, laments the resistance to change with which the aging Corporation still struggles. Highfield, who heads the Corporation's hugely successful website BBC: helps old-media content producers transfer their ideas across media.

> The BBC used to be frightened of giving power to users. But new media creates communities which replace the kind of communities which the BBC has proudly built in the past. Linear broadcasting pushes out content, delivering it to people with very little in the way of allowing them to interact. There were guidelines at the BBC about *not* letting users contribute, but nothing at the time about how we can open it up and allow them to do so.

Reith's 1936 reluctance to listen to customers is a long time dying.

CHECKLIST: REACHING THE AUDIENCE

- Know the audience: what are you making, and for whom? If you're making something for yourself (which is fine), identify the maximum audience you'll get. It affects budgeting.
- Research concepts where you can, and refine the proposition. But don't stifle creativity unduly.
- Use business judgement to incorporate or ignore research data. The audience has no reference point to provide guidance on original content that has yet to be created.
- Spot existing audience habits and take preferred slot to encourage trials.
- This is the age of continuous partial attention: audiences consume more content than ever, because they do more than one thing at a time. To really grab their attention, use many media.
- High-profile content franchises attract existing fans while also drawing in newcomers.

REFERENCES

David Buckingham, *Public Secrets: Eastenders and its Audience*, BFI, 1987.

Andrew Crissell, *Understanding Radio*, Routledge, 1994.

Ehrenberg, Goodheart and Barwise, 'Double Jeopardy Revisited', *Journal of Marketing*, 1990.

Jacques Horovitch and Michele J. Panak, *Total Customer Satisfaction*, Pitman, 1992.

FORMULAIC AND ORIGINALITY: THE TENSIONS WITHIN

6

'When forced to work within a strict framework the imagination is taxed to its utmost – and will produce the richest ideas. Given total freedom the work is likely to sprawl.'

TS Eliot

William Shakespeare knew a good formula when he saw one. Here is a man whose job was to deliver an audience, the biggest one possible for his medium – the theatre – and extract the highest possible value from it. Shakespeare's content has enjoyed return visits for 400 years. He may not necessarily have thought in terms of cost per acquisition or lifetime customer value, but as a businessman Shakespeare satisfied audiences by combining creative and business disciplines.

This most distinguished playwright was far from the most original of writers. Shakespeare selected stories and ideas, even whole chunks of dialogue, from others who had gone before, amending them as required to suit his own purpose. An early multi-tasker, this one man in his time played many parts. Actor, writer, producer, impresario. It is sometimes said that if he were alive today, Shakespeare would be writing for television. He wanted to achieve big audiences, and that's what TV delivers.

No doubt he would now be dabbling in interactive storytelling if broadband connections had reached Elizabethan London. In fact, many of Shakespeare's plays have been adapted to digital media, with educational software bringing characters, dialogue and settings to life.

He remains a guaranteed box-office hit. Repertory theatres across the world play to halls half full, if that, for many new plays. Stick on *Hamlet* and bums meet seats.

Now, if the greatest English playwright in history was happy to borrow many stories, rather than create everything from scratch, why is it that formulaic content is so maligned by critics? Anything produced from a formula is easy, goes the argument. It's been done before. It's safe, boring. Can't they think of anything new to say?

Formulaic content is, if one believes newspaper critics, a very bad thing.

If this were a mathematics book, we could rustle up a few formulae, present a range of problems to which they can be applied, and everyone would think, 'How useful', and go off with a spring in their step, happy at finding guaranteed solutions to tricky sums. Formulae are good for maths. They don't endure the criticism borne by their artistic cousins.

But artistic formulae work too – for audiences who know what they like and are happy to have more, for producers who have at least some guidelines that work to follow, and for distributors who have a better chance of backing winning beetles? No artistic formula is guaranteed to work, but the balance of probabilities swings the right way when content producers find the essence of a form within a formula – taking those elements with which audiences identify, and into which they are willing to invest their time, and transforming the form with something surprising and original.

So although Shakespeare borrowed his storylines from others, and manipulated the conventions of drama, his talent lay in bringing new insights, usually into what it is to be human, to his stories. Once he had mastered his art, his productions became sticky.

For twenty-first-century content producers, manufacturing hit content to a predetermined formula may sound easier than chancing an arm with completely original content, but neither extreme is likely to please an audience. Seen-it-all-before content presents the audience with little incentive for repeat visits. Producers may get away with a single hit, but if repeat visits are what makes a business, then that is never enough. And at the opposite end, the more creative, beautiful, unusual, bizarre, introspective, esoteric material satisfies only the creators. That's not a great business proposition either.

Finding the guaranteed banker of a formula is never easy. For formulae in art are never as precise as formulae in science. Their essence may be inappropriate to transfer to other media or new forms of content, and one would never know why. The form within the formula – the individual elements that can be repackaged to create something fresh – is more valuable than the formula itself. Form contains the conventions that audiences understand, but are flexible enough for surprise, drama, originality to be built upon them. The resulting new content may veer towards formulaic, but not in a negative sense. Formulae work because they are reassuring and familiar. Done right – remaining true to the form, but spicing it up with intuition, immersion and imagination – they keep audiences coming back. The quest for addictive formulae is based on respect for form.

REPLAYING FAMILIAR FAVOURITES

Wallowing in nostalgia isn't the preserve of the old. If you've ever found yourself recalling television programmes of your childhood, you will remember them fondly, even as their limitations now become apparent – towering monsters that are clearly only the size of actors in foil lizard costumes, or puppets that were patently that and nothing more. It all seemed so real at the time.

Audiences are attracted to familiar favourites: old stories retold, and told well. If you're trying to lure children to your content, delighting parents is a good place to start. Parents can't resist telling children of their own childhood, and commending favourite old stories can result in a new generation of addicts.

There are two main ways of bringing old content to new audiences – the more costly, vibrant version of bringing the story up to date, using new technologies, graphics and sound effects to fit the tale into the twenty-first-century. In musical terms, this is the cover version. The alternative is to dig into the archive and replay the original – the reissue.

One doesn't need to go back too many years to discover old material for a new market. Finding content to recall the formative years of any target audience of today is relatively easy. It's usually at the front of the archive, not the back. For most people, nostalgia isn't about anything that happened before the Second World War. And much is very recent indeed.

If most digital media are consumed by the relatively young – those, say, under 40 – then the key periods are between about 10 and 30 years ago. For people aged 50, nostalgia is what happened 30 years ago or more. If you're 60, it's 40 years ago. And for people in their early twenties, one only needs to recreate the stories from less than a decade ago. Nostalgia is thinking about being young.

The beauty of nostalgic content is that it doesn't need too much imagination. Pick a date, look in the papers to find out what was going on, and repackage it.

Whole communities of interest can be created through building repositories of nostalgic content, which audiences not only want to consume but to which they enjoy contributing too. Friends Reunited is a classmates' contact site that is frighteningly addictive. With a bulletin board, classified listings and a chance to contact people you've been trying to forget, the content is almost self-perpetuating. Recognizing that demand for nostalgia goes back to childhood, Friends Reunited revives memories from recent history, not ancient. Most of its users left school in the past 20 years, with fewer people listed from the 1950s or before – though, interestingly, old boys of a number of schools claim to have left in 1901, making them about 115 years old. Even audiences of non-fiction websites create fiction.

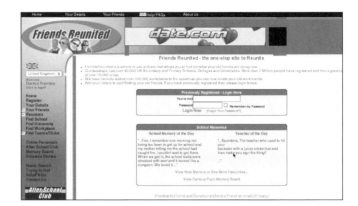

FriendsReunited.co.uk: nostalgia is thinking about being young.

Source: www.friendsreunited.co.uk

The beauty of nostalgic content is that it doesn't need too much imagination. Pick a date, look in the papers to find out what was going on, and repackage it. Quick, simple, cheap. It's perfect digital content – as long as it's told well with the audience in mind. Cynical reselling of content that audiences already own may result in sales, but perhaps not goodwill. Consumers may have been prepared to replace vinyl records with CDs on the basis of improved sound quality, but many resent the high cost. At the same time, they've been willing to buy the same recordings packaged in new ways.

The Beatles' *1* album was the Christmas hit of 2000, which repackaged old material with a strong theme – the history of a great band's number-one records and nothing else. That's a story. But try selling half-baked nostalgia – an old artist without his old repertoire, for example – and audiences may not be all that keen to follow, because it's not nostalgia, just a new piece of content. It may work, or it may not, even if it has some of the elements for success. Cliff Richard singing 'Over the Rainbow' is not wholly nostalgic. It's just Sir Cliff banging out an old classic. The package has two strong elements, the song and the star, but arguably is not a cohesive whole. Robbie Williams swinging his way through 1950s' tunes is not wholly nostalgic either, being similarly just the star and the songs. But Robbie has the advantage because of his active CD-buying fan base at the time of release. He's the new star with old songs, but with much of the material new to his audience, he presents a fresh twist to tested material and a reason to buy. While Cliff sells only to Cliff fans in the main, Robbie's sales are broader – to his own fans and an older audience who like the older songs.

There's no such thing as half-nostalgic. Only old talent and old content together creates true nostalgia, as Chrysalis Records found when launching a suite of 'heritage acts' – classic (sometimes a euphemism for old) bands producing new albums, with new material, which few people bought. The label's chief executive lamented: 'People like going to see them play in concert, because they like to be reminded of all those great songs from years ago and probably own them all already. These people are less interested in new product' (*Music Week*, 2001). Nostalgia has to be content as the audience remembers it. It can't be only part of the story – however good that part is. Presenting something old by someone new, or vice versa, creates something new, not nostalgic.

There is a growing appetite for very recent history. These are the stories of our grandparents, within the living memory of many. Catering for this market, the US Arts & Entertainment network has transferred historical content across media, creating a hit property. In addition to telling narrative stories on television, it owns geneaology.com, helping people trace family trees, and *Biography* magazine. With cross-media promotion, and great storytelling content, it has built a community of users with a shared interest in recent history.

For history is something we all share in common. It is the biggest-selling non-fiction genre in the book trade, does a fair trade in television series, and is a staple resource for movies and novels. You only have to turn to Shakespeare again to see a reliance on the power struggles of European monarchs. Retelling the stories of recent history is a small industry in its own right. There's even a market in battlefield tours. A company called Holts escorts tourists – if that's not too flippant a word for people who pay homage with genuinely respectful intent – around the former trenches of Flanders.

While the Arts & Entertainment Network may carry other strands of programming on its main television network, whole channels – on television and the Internet – have sprung up dedicated to history. 'What happened on this day in history' are popular columns in newspapers, with counterparts on radio, and now on the Web too. The History Channel, for example, gives almost one-quarter of its home page to anniversary items.

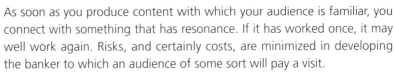

MATCHING AUDIENCE EXPECTATIONS

As soon as you produce content with which your audience is familiar, you connect with something that has resonance. If it has worked once, it may well work again. Risks, and certainly costs, are minimized in developing the banker to which an audience of some sort will pay a visit.

You have the characters, the settings, the history. All it needs is a slight new spin, a newish plot, and a bit of marketing to the same old audience. So *Rocky* reappears in *Rocky II*, *III* and *IV*. Critically, the sequels may not be up to much, but that's not the point, nice though it would be. The business aim is to keep people coming back and to make more money than you spend.

In a world with so much available content, successful old stories are branding tools. With more channels available across more platforms, spanning all forms of entertainment, the stories audiences have heard before, and liked, are much more certain to attract customers again. Just as people seek out the reassurance and familiarity of favoured brands, so they do with content.

This is the end of the formulaic scale in which few surprises are permitted. Content is sticky because it matches audience expectations completely. If, in the next film of the *Rocky* series, Rocky were to find his true vocation as a ballerina, the audience, expecting a bit of a punch-up and the pleasures of the boxing ring somewhere along the line, would probably feel somewhat cheated. The next film in the series would almost certainly be doomed. Mismanage audience expectations and business will fall.

Playwrights from Shakespeare through Ibsen and Ayckbourn have understood the importance of managing customers' expectations. Posters, flyers, programmes set some kind of context, so the audience knows what they're letting themselves in for. Complete surprises may not necessarily be good ones. It's as well to know that *Ghosts* is a domestic drama, or that *Anthony and Cleopatra* is a tragedy, not a romp. So the author thoughtfully adds a qualifying note to the title of their work. It is the responsibility of the content producer to provide guidance, not for the audience to guess.

The ideal is to create something refreshingly original, but within a familiar context. These are genres with which audiences identify – in film, for example, they would be action movies, spaghetti westerns, period dramas. In music, they are classical, or dance, or rock, or blues. In novels, they are romance, thrillers, or contemporary fiction. Customers know what they are buying before they buy, and understand the conventions of the form. There's still plenty of room to disappoint or overwhelm. But no one can say they didn't know what to expect.

Even producers who have no truck with the rigidity of rules nonetheless wish to carry their audience along with them, which means following recognized conventions. Speaking about his 2001 period drama *Gosford Park*, movie director Robert Altman said, 'If you're trying to create something original, you don't follow rules. You only follow rules if you want to create something that's already been done before.' Altman claims rarely to think of the audience during the production process. With strong foundations laid in a great script, the story should tell itself and great stories find audiences.

Gosford Park, which cost $20 million, modest in comparison with Hollywood blockbusters, and the first feature film screenplay of writer Julian Fellowes, attracted a cast of knights and dames of British theatre and film. A hugely complex script, with multiple storylines, it was a critical success. Should the producers desire, there is scope for a novel, a board game, and a TV series (the return of 1960s series *Upstairs Downstairs*, perhaps?). Altman's ability to discard rules and create something original is only partly true. A master of his form, the conventions of linear storytelling remain in his work.

Robert Jones, chief of the Film Council's Premiere Fund, which supported *Gosford Park*, commented in *Screen International* (24 August 2001): 'When you are looking for something that might work, you look for something that is both familiar and original.' *Gosford Park* achieves the balance by finding its place on the continuum. It veers towards Altman's preference for the original, but recognizes that finances follow projects that stand a decent chance of getting seen. If that's a bit too cynical, *Gosford Park* is also a cracking good product – fine story, genius director, all-star cast, put together by craftsmen of the first order. Altman's contention is that when you have a story so good, you create a great piece without recourse to tired formulas. Audiences want to see great things.

Though creative business is original business, in *Gosford Park's* case, the audience returns to the nostalgic period between the two world wars. Wars, being painful, are especially nostalgic. In fact, the roots of the word nostalgia are related to pain and a desire for home – from *nostos* (a return to one's native land) and *algos*, meaning pain or distress. The French equivalent is *maladie du pays*, the Spanish *mal de corazon*. First identified by seventeenth-century Swiss physician Johannes Hofer, it originally referred to young soldiers who had lost all hope of ever returning home. 'They become sad, taciturn, listless, solitary, full of sighs and moans' wrote Dr Hofer (quoted in Le Fance, 2002). Which is what happens to audiences when formulaic content is poorly produced.

Nostalgia is also addictive. Pain releases adrenaline and endorphins, and while pain hurts, the rush of bodily chemicals makes it pleasurable too. And that's the feeling when nostalgic content is done well.

'WHERE WERE YOU WHEN ... ?' MOMENTS

People flock to nostalgic content because it grounds them in a time and a place, uniting them in a community. Audiences like the familiar.

Music in particular has the power to place us at a moment in time. News events manage it occasionally – the 'where were you when … ?' moments. Where were you when JFK got shot, Elvis died, man first walked on the moon, or the Twin Towers came down?

But music, being only a few minutes long, gets played repeatedly in a relatively short period of time and, being mobile, is heard indoors and out. Tracks become associated with events of a period. Entire radio stations are programmed around musical timespans, often defined by decades – 'We play the hits of the 80s and the 90s' – as much as musical genres. The clamour to recreate a period in time rather than any love for a particular type of music attracts audiences wanting to remember a time in their lives.

The essence of a formula is that it provides a definitive answer if a set of rules is followed. Audiences come back because they know what to expect. In seeking their loyalty, surprises must be limited.

Top-40 radio, one of the most popular radio formats, contains no surprises at all in its purest form. And a top-ten station presents just about the narrowest range of sticky content around. Relying on others to break hits, these stations pick up the ten best-selling records, or those at the top of airtime charts, and rotate them endlessly. The point at which listeners choose to turn off is assumed to generally follow the tenth song, when the cycle starts over again. The stations are happy because average listening time is about ten songs' worth, with advertising and sponsorship messages getting to a very specific, if somewhat musically unsophisticated, audience.

At its most extreme, this would lead to content of a very narrow range of material, and an average user time that is very short indeed. A top-one station, on which only one hit song is played over and over again, would have average access time of a single song. Presumably, there are songs that are in such demand that audiences want to hear them repeatedly, at least for a little while.

In the UK, a local authority took legal action against a resident who was causing unnecessary distress to her neighbours by blasting Whitney Houston's theme from *The Bodyguard*, 'I will always love you', loud, late and constantly. Once the track ended, back on the turntable it went. Again and again. A psychologist gave evidence that Whitney's bassline was too addictive and the errant householder therefore couldn't help her actions. She wasn't alone in her fondness for Whitney, although her neighbours clearly weren't fans. In addition to sales of the single, a number-one hit across the world, *The Bodyguard* soundtrack still stands as one of the most successful movie tie-in CDs, with sales in excess of 30 million. The film promotes the song, and the song promotes the film. Sticky content transfers.

The most popular content at any moment in time will, by definition, get the biggest audience. But a massive audience that sticks around for the shortest amount of time may not be financially viable. There's little time to cross-promote, introduce new content, and deliver advertising or other ways to make the content pay.

When content selection is overly formulaic – in this case, playing only the number-one record of the moment – no room is left for creative judgement. Clearly, where the formula is so restrictive that it might prevent the audience from returning rather than helping to build it, the formula is bad. The number-one record changes regularly, and not everyone likes the number one each week. When a melodic ballad at the peak of the charts is bumped off by an aggressive rapper with a penchant for chainsaws, the likelihood of both records appealing to the same audience is small. The four-minute user who doesn't come back is clearly not a great business prospect. And quite frankly, short, repetitive, singular content won't do an awful lot for one's creative credibility.

Most content providers seek to be credible as well as commercially successful, and excessive repeats prevent refreshment and renewal, ultimately limiting audience size. If you're not too hung up about the need for credibility, formulas work well – especially for content that is short, reliable and constantly available. If you're about to undertake a journey and need travel news, for example, it's useful to be able to go to a website, or a broadcaster, or a travel company, and be guaranteed that the news you need will be accessible when you need it.

If you need to relax, it's handy to know where to find classical music – or dance music, or live webcams of goldfish, if that's what you use to relax. If it's repetitive, that doesn't matter, as long as it delivers as expected. Even ambient music, once the preserve of elevators and supermarkets, sells moderately well, which at first looked like producers having a bit of a laugh. Cassettes of whales or birdsong can be bought in authentic music shops as well as garage forecourts. Content that is undemanding, repetitive and delivers as promised sells well.

INTERMEDIARIES FILTER ORIGINAL CONTENT

At the opposite end of the scale to narrow content that delivers as promised is the highly original – or content with such breadth that the audience hasn't a clue what's coming next, or whether they will like it. This is a riskier option for producers and audience alike.

Let's stick with the music example. Let's say you have a million tracks of music from which to compile a CD, radio playlist or online streamed service, and yet no creative judgement is to be made about which to select when. If this was a radio station, then it would be one in which the same song never got played twice. Good songs would come round very seldom, because there are more poor records than there are great ones – evidence, once again, of the diversity of creative business. The audience would quickly realize that the content is variable in quality, and that much isn't very good at all. They need a filter, an editor, to help them select between the good and the bad. It sounds patronizing, and it's the antithesis of the personalized nirvana that digital is meant to have delivered. But we can't all consume everything, and we tend to crave more of what we like. So we need help to avoid the chaff among the wheat.

Even when making scheduling decisions themselves, creating personalized schedules according to individual musical tastes, audiences find it useful to have another opinion to ease the selection process. Intermediaries could be friends or trusted advisers such as music critics. Even so, the chances are that only a small proportion of available tracks will be selected regularly, and most will remain unheard, gaining virtual dust. According to Jupiter Research, by 2001, 40% of European Internet users were downloading music, 18 million people had bought music online, and 40% were willing to pay a small fee to hear commercial-free music. Hearing new music, sometimes personally selected, sometimes chosen by expert schedulers, is something audiences continue to want, and for which they are prepared to pay. But those creating highly original material, distributing it without the help of an intermediary, will find building a sizable audience difficult.

If there is a continuum between formulaic, narrow, carefully selected content on the one hand, and the highly original, unfiltered flow on the other, few people will enjoy content for long at either extreme. There's a role for both original content and formulaic content, but at its extremes there is probably not much of a demand from an audience sufficiently large, who stick around sufficiently long, and who will make it pay. Audiences resist anything too formulaic for long because they feel manipulated. What is fun for a while becomes boring after repeated doses. But present content that is too alien and audiences won't be able to engage with it, and they will have no shared emotional history with the subject matter or characters or sounds. For longevity, content needs to be pitched between the two extremes.

The choice of positioning along the formulaic–original continuum will vary with both the kind of content business producers are in (music being more radical and original than news production, for example), and on the profile of the target audience – their age, how cosmopolitan they are, and so on. Some audiences are more accepting of highly original material than others. Younger people adapt to more innovative content faster than older audiences, but at the same time they define their range of preferences quite narrowly. Young people may consume only one or two genres of music – hip-hop or nu-metal, for example – but they expect to hear lots of new tracks. They demand depth more than breadth – a tight formula aimed at their interests, with surprises and new material within it.

CONTENT FRANCHISES

Content that establishes a large audience by following recognizable conventions, but that has elements that are transferable and unique, can become the stickiest content of all. The digital era has seen the emergence of global content franchises – materials that transfer across media and markets, and that retain key characteristics wherever they go. This is material that sticks to a formula, but acts local when transferred. This seriously addictive content attracts the biggest audience when it becomes a brand in its own right – recognizable, trustworthy, consistent content. Franchised content is defining content and can attract new audiences to distribution channels.

When AOL Time Warner bought the rights to all seven Harry Potter stories, four of them were yet to be written. The old-cum-new media conglomerate wanted exclusive rights to content across all its distribution outlets, not just the rights to seven films. At the time of the deal, nothing came bigger than Harry Potter. With 115 million books sold before the first film opened, the pre-existing fan base was probably larger than that for any previous movie. For its estimated $500 million, AOL Time Warner bought the rights to seven, presumably hit, movies for its Warner Brothers studio, together with a franchise extending across the group's businesses. The soundtrack was cut by Atlantic Records label, part of Warner Music, and AOL websites and Time Warner's magazines gained access to the most powerfully addictive content on the planet.

The clever part of the Harry Potter deal is that AOL owns more than the rights to create branded content. They also have licensing and merchandising rights, providing a cut in the extension of the franchise into other properties. Most of the movie's production costs were underwritten by other commercial deals, including one of the world's biggest sponsorship programmes, a £150 million global marketing rights agreement with Coca-Cola. AOL Time Warner benefits from sales of Lego Hogwarts classrooms and Quidditch board games. Online, Harry Potter fans can access quizzes, discussion forums, a *Daily Prophet* update, chances to download scenes from the movie, and a wizard shop. Whatever the medium, there's a piece of Harry Potter to go with it.

That the author insists on maintaining a veto over commercial exploitation of her creation bodes both good and bad for AOL Time Warner. JK Rowling's determination in securing an all-British cast for the film will have kept a lid on the astronomical talent fees demanded by the world's biggest movie stars – the audience in this case demanding authentic representation of the original story rather than a sparkling cast. But Rowling also forced restraint on the exploitation of commercial partnerships – the art being more important than the money.

If earning money was all-important, more important than the magic of the story, Rowling would have followed the Star Wars franchise route. Anything and everything that could be sold would be sold. Instead, Time Warner AOL licensed far fewer products than usual for a blockbuster film, particularly one for children. Some of the more common hit movie partnerships were completely excluded – there is no Harry Potter burger, for example.

Ralph Ardill, director at creative agency Imagination, explains:

> Rowling realises that if she doesn't have control, the whole magic of what she has created will be deconstructed to the lowest possible denominator and it will lose its mystery. The more you make the story real, for example, with little plastic toys with faces of the children in the film, the more you have lost the power of imagination.

Instead, there are a few powerful deals, ones that will generate revenues and extend the franchise but that protect the story, characters and imagination of the audience. With seven stories in the series, the story and the franchise must not burn out early. The core medium is the book, but the integrity of the story across all other media is paramount if the Potter proposition is not to be diminished. Being imaginative and a global brand, Lego works for Harry Potter. Being transitory and split into domestic markets, ice-cream doesn't.

Coke and Harry Potter are two giants among franchises, says Ardill:

> … the self-proclaimed greatest marketer in the world teaming up with the most powerful author. She clearly has a few more books left in her, so there is a long-term interest in maintaining control. That control probably creates a smaller franchise than it otherwise could be. But the author has veto, and for her the most important aspect is being true to her story.

LOCKING-IN TALENT

The cost of talent can play havoc with economic models of creative businesses, because talent creates substantial value but is generally not employed directly by the content producer. So there is no control on a key resource that adds value to the business. Hiring key talent with strong track records who are recognized by large audiences is another way to minimize risk. These people attract audiences by their name alone.

Pearl Harbor, a critical disaster of a disaster movie, which cost $130 million to make but grossed $200 million, was more of a creative than a financial disappointment. It continues to earn revenues as it progresses through the distribution chain of video and DVD, through cable and satellite television, and eventually to free-to-air broadcasters. Its value through the chain depends on a movie's initial success – for it is the excitement it originally produced that will drive demand from audiences who never made it into the cinema. But with the film a creative disappointment, arguably the biggest media equity created by the movie was for its lead Josh Hartnett, a young, and to that point undistinguished, actor. *Pearl Harbor* brought Hartnett to the attention of probably smaller audiences than producing studio Touchstone Pictures had hoped, but the well-hyped blockbuster and a decent performance did get him noticed by other studios. Touchstone paid him well, yet has no financial interest in his future earnings.

If talent has control, then the challenge for business is to control the talent. Managing talent, retaining key staff, is no easy task – particularly when it concerns creative people who have little inclination to be managed and little concern about toeing corporate lines. When the only real scarce resource is talent, their contentment becomes a central management task.

Most creative people are extroverts; indeed, some are loud extroverts with strong opinions. Results of psychometric tests from Myers Briggs show that 75% of people who have taken their tests (usually business-people) are extroverts. Now there is evidence that these extroverts are taking over the world. As children are placed in nurseries at a younger age, and as families move around the country or globe, they have to adapt to being outside the family much earlier in life. Research by Dr Raj Persaud on the rise of extroversion concludes that this is a change from a time when children were required to be seen and not heard, into a world in which they are expected to speak their minds and be assertive.

Although creative industries have always been riddled with extroverts, they have now taken a grip on the whole business world. And it's not just that there are going to be more extroverts in circulation. They are gaining in potency too. Extroverts in future will be more extrovert than they are today. By 2010, college-age students are expected to be almost twice as extrovert as students in the 1960s (Twenge, 2001). For committed intro-verts, this is concerning. They are a dying breed.

Creative talent is demanding not only because of the higher incidence of aggressive extrover-sion, but because of their accompanying insecurities. Like the businesses for which they work, most creative people seek the biggest audi-ence for their art, and, if they have a business head on them too, a decent share of the profit.

Star artists, or very talented ones (they're not always the same thing), transfer their stories across media. Boxers play pantomime, footballers host talk shows, novelists turn to serialization on the Internet, comic book heroes move into film. When the transfer works – and often it doesn't – its value increases hugely, but only to a point. Knowing when overexposure reduces value, rather than adds to it, is the job of managers.

With the right exposure and proper management, talent develops equity, a value that is profitable to the artist and to everyone else along the production value chain.

With the right exposure and proper management, talent develops equity, a value that is profitable to the artist and to everyone else along the production value chain. Audiences seek out named artists. On the whole, they show unfathomable loyalty to talent with strong equity, and to the stories with which they are linked. Audiences are less enamoured with faceless producers and distributors.

The equity that the biggest talent possesses has a value that is best kept out of the hands of competitors, although this is less true when producers or distributors have invested in sufficient marketing on the underlying content to build the franchise regardless of the star. Audiences then have loyalties on numerous levels – to the channel, to the content or programme, and to the artist. So the star player in a football team may have a fan base to match the team for which he plays. But if he falls out of favour, it may still be worth holding on to him to keep him away from leading competitors where he may turn his talents against his old pals. While he is away from the audience, his equity diminishes. That's a problem if he's an asset on the balance sheet, but it is easier if the club invests in its own brand development and has a fan base more addicted to the club than its players. Better all round, though, if stars are kept happy, though that probably means costs spiralling ever upwards.

So a formula for creating stickiness inevitably includes locking in creative talent, especially talent that attracts a huge audience. When audiences have so much choice, names they know and trust are more likely to get their attention than the unknown and untested. If you can get Tom Cruise to post material to your website or perform in your advert, you should be able to do quite good business because Tom Cruise has a large fan base. Endorsements by big stars in advertisements are powerful sales tools, which is why newscasters are prevented from starring in commercials in many countries. They are just too famous, too authoritative, their talents arguably too transferable, that audiences may believe that the truth of a commercial message matches the truth of the news.

Television channels and record companies buy lengthy contracts of star acts to keep a regular flow of high-quality material flowing. Long, exclusive contracts also keep talent out of the hands of the competition. Everyone should be happy – distributor, artist and audience. But sometimes it goes spectacularly wrong, with content creators locked into deals with stars they no longer want to use just to keep them out of the jaws of competitors. Occasionally, the talent no longer wants to play, as when singer George Michael famously refused to record for his contracted label Sony Music, which he felt hadn't given enough support to his albums 'Listen Without Prejudice' and 'Red, Hot and Dance'. Michael asked the high court to force Sony to release him from his contract – but he lost his argument that the contract amounted to a restraint of trade. Although Sony didn't get a note out of Michael for a fallow five years, the artist was unable to defect to a competing label.

George Michael's career was ultimately affected little by his silent years. Most other talent, though, requires constant nurturing, lest the audience has its attention diverted by newcomers. The value of talent declines quickly when it lies dormant. So those with a limited shelf life extract value while they can.

Former England soccer captain Alan Shearer, in his early thirties, is working on his second autobiography, after the success of *My Story so Far*. David Beckham's wife, Victoria, published hers at the age of 26. Singer Ronan Keating, who also produced his life story in his twenties, upset many young fans when an updated, cheaper, paperback version appeared just months later, complete with new content, which addicted fans felt they just had to buy – again. What appears exploitative, or naive to some, is the artist's prudent transfer of their story and timing is important. The value of talent ebbs and flows, and autobiographies are most likely to be read when interest in the author is at its height. In most cases, that is unlikely to be at the very end of a long, well-lived life. Content that is fading in the minds of the audience needs refreshing before transfer.

SPRUCING UP OLD CONTENT

It's true to say that some big-name content seems to go on forever. But for most, there is a natural lifespan that, unless the content is able to reinvent itself to be relevant to each passing period (it's not even a generation), or tells such a pertinent, emotionally charged story that endures – such as *Casablanca* in film or 'My Way' in music – then it will die. It may rise to the level of cult, like *Prisoner Cell Block H* (small, somewhat weird audience), or even *Star Wars* (massive, somewhat weird audience). Everyone else needs to create new stories for the time the present ones run out of steam.

Whether you are a footballer, a pop star, a television series, or a transferable film, generally you can expect to attract an audience for a few years at most without reinventing yourself. Other strings to the bow make you transferable. Transferable football stars become coaches or pundits. Pop stars become producers or managers. Film-makers have new projects in their portfolios. All build upon the lessons they have learned and the talents with which they are blessed.

The advertising community knows better than most how to do this. Just as more creative content is instantly forgettable, so is most advertising. But when an advertisement works, it can run forever – provided it remains original and relevant. When it doesn't, it's time to change. Until 2002, UK tea PG Tips had used a family of tea-swilling chimpanzees to sell tea bags (and previously tea leaves). They lasted more than 45 years. Each commercial was a mini-drama, a panache of monkey business, and Britons took to PG Tips, but more especially the advertisements – even as the tea market declined and people turned to sodas and bottled waters. From time to time, Unilever thought the brand messages were, no longer relevant to the younger generation – which is always a downer for a brand, and a time when new advertising concepts are likely to be commissioned. The chimps had been replaced once before, but they were quickly un-retired. In 2001, Unilever's product managers considered storytelling longevity to equate to an out-of-touch brand, so they reinvented it to face twenty-first-century beverage battles.

Advertisers monitor not just overall sales of products but also the effects of advertising upon those sales. Once commercials show signs of slipping, new ads should have been pre-tested and be ready to roll. It's no good waiting for the work to alienate the audience, for by then there will be no customers left. It's the same for developing creative content. If the audience has been enticed away by more exciting material, or worse, has left of their own accord, then that's the fault of producers running content into the ground without freshening it up and keeping it relevant.

THE BEAUTY AND THE HAZARDS OF FORMULAS IN BUSINESS

Formulas help in all types of business. They form the shorthand by which work should get done faster, although at the extreme, formats are bureaucracies, where every procedure is defined, just as in the most stringent franchise operation. Even organizations that speak the language of empowerment seek control. It's good corporate communications, they say.

Being 'on message', speaking with one voice, ensuring the people pull together in the same direction.

But control and creativity are not natural bedfellows. Workers at Mars Confectionery, right up until the 1990s, had to wear navy suits and crisp, white shirts. Rebel and the slippery slope of chocolate career progression was blocked. Uniform at Mars matched that of a good grammar school. It was not alone – the dress code at IBM ran along much the same lines, eventually succumbing to pressures from the more relaxed talent magnet of Silicon Valley. In the financial districts of the UK, pinstripes died harder; well-cut navy suits hang on in Wall Street, and business style prevails in European financial capitals.

Conformity begets standards, and standards reflect upon organizations. Yet uniformity leads to a loss of self. The dotcom era did for suits in traditional industries such as banking and accountancy, certainly for a time. Some men may never wear a tie to work again. At the time, some clothes shops, particularly those stocking formal wear, found precious sales slipping away. Austin Reed, at the upper end of the market, and a plentiful supplier of pinstripes and chalk stripes, suffered a share-price collapse and rushed in a team of trendier designers (just in time for dotcoms to die, creating a small rally for interview suits).

There has been a slackening off of dress codes – the appearance of giving greater freedom to the workforce – yet at the same time an increased desire for conformity of message: controlling output. Ralph Ardill at Imagination says:

> The concept of the living brand and the culture change which is talked about in business today is quite frightening. You walk through the door and suddenly you are a Microsoft person, for example. And this means you dress like this and you think like that and you are given the Microsoft version of the Koran when you arrive. It starts to erode your ability to improvise and interpret and imagine.

Mircosoft, Mars and IBM are significant, successful organizations that value creativity. Yet there's a discontinuity between what many creative businesses say and what they do. What they broadcast to outsiders and how they communicate with employees are worlds apart. Compare the money and effort that go into producing glossy television and magazine commercials with the resources that go into communicating with employees – done at worst through tacky notice boards and at best through email, intranets and 'town-hall' meetings. Organizations may say that their people are their most valuable asset, but few take as much care of their internal communications as they do with their advertising and promotions.

CHECKLIST: MAKING IT STICKY

- Limit the surprises: predictability is best.
- Any surprises should be nice surprises, within the context of what people expect.
- Don't follow rules slavishly – you will end up creating something so undifferentiated that there will be little reason to visit your content rather than that of your competitors.
- Transform the 'form' in 'formulaic' with something surprising and original.
- The more niche the content, the more enthusiastic the audience will be (if you can guarantee your survival).
- Build trust in what you do, then deliver the content you promise.
- As you shouldn't follow rules slavishly, you should now ignore everything in this summary.
- Manage the equity in talent.
- Lock in creative talent with a contract that sticks them to you.
- Lavish the same care on internal communications as you do with the outside world.

REFERENCES

James Le Fance, 'In sickness and in health', *Sunday Telegraph*, 14 April 2002.

Music Week, 'Papillon bows our heritage as veterans struggle for sales', 1 December 2001.

J.M. Twenge, 'Birth cohort changes in extroversion', *Personality and Individual Differences*, **30**(5), 2001.

DISTRIBUTION MAKES CONTENT PAY

7

'The future is already here. It is just unevenly distributed.'

William Gibson, science fiction writer

Creating sticky hit property, the addictive content that keeps audiences coming back for more, and across many media, is rarely easy. It requires many skills. A spark of original genius and the management of diverse artists and craftspeople. Effective marketing and technological expertise. Secure finance and not a little bit of luck. Most fundamentally, a true hit property requires mass distribution. A partnership with someone who is going to get the content in front of audiences. Without it, all efforts are wasted.

In the multiband, multimedia world, massive distribution needs a massive distributor. Although technology is now relatively inexpensive, and Web distribution available to all, without the support of a leading distributor, audiences are almost certainly destined to remain small. Stand-alone websites are by no means cheap. The best are costly to produce and maintain. Even success leads to financial conundrums – the more customers who come to a site, the more it costs to keep it live and efficient. More servers, more bandwidth, more cost.

Self-distribution may now be possible, but to make a business of addictive content distributors are crucial. A film-maker without a distributor haemorrhages cash with little hope of seeing a return – although those who really feel the need to tell their story in celluloid spurn digital for old-fashioned film processing and tout their reels to film clubs.

Here's the maths that show how narrow distribution limits content creation. Say there are 250 film clubs willing to take a movie, each with 100 members paying a £5 entry fee, with a 30% cut of the box office going to the producer. That's £37,500 gross revenue. Such a minor film might expect £15,000 from a cable television screening. Try making a blockbuster (and a profit) with that. The miracle is that masochistic audiences are prepared to sit through low-budget content, regardless of quality, professing to the enjoyment of art. Creativity may not be wholly dependent on finance, but the greatest productions usually are.

Whatever the genre or medium, regardless of the strength of the content, or the size of the potential audience, if there is no way to distribute the work widely, and in a place to which people come, then the marketing costs associated with going it alone are likely to be large. Of course, many people with a story to tell do have the courage of their convictions and publish with their own money, or raise relatively small amounts of finance. Art-house cinemas attract a loyal band of followers, and a sizable number of films just about cover their costs. Authors who feel they have a book in them that leading publishing houses have been foolish enough to turn down stump up the money and have it printed themselves. Publish and be damned. Most are.

BANDWIDTH EXPLOSION MEANS MORE OF THE MEDIOCRE

Although it may be a personal achievement, self-publication isn't true success and isn't so much addictive content as addictive publishing. Vanity publishing builds neither the hit nor the hit property. Rarely is material that distributors have declined to back transferable across many media. Vanity is fine, if that is the limit of your ambitions. But if you want to build transferable, sticky content, then someone else, someone big, needs to believe in the power of your story and your ability to bring it to life.

if you want to build transferable, sticky content, then someone else, someone big, needs to believe in the power of your story and your ability to bring it to life.

Vanity publishing, once the preserve of exploitative printers happy to produce books for the hard of writing, is now in the professional, big-business league. It doesn't go by the name of vanity, and it is no longer the exclusive provenance of the deluded. With distributive power concentrated increasingly in a few big companies, whether distributing music, books, television, Internet or all of these, distributors find that they don't always have to pay for content. Instead, they can charge for access.

Want to launch your own television channel? Unheard of unless you've got billions in the bank? No longer. Cheaper technology, enhanced bandwidth and lighter regulation put the ambition within reach of even small businesses. Hire a transponder, knock a few programmes together, and you're on the air. While still costly, it is no longer completely out of the question. So many companies want to be on television, even for a small amount of time, that if you find the right programming formula, you may even be able to sublet airtime. By charging for access to your schedules, you may not even have the troublesome problem of attracting viewers, provided someone else is happy to stump up enough money to get on air and make you profitable. It's the model used by classified advertising magazines – free to users, but the person selling their car has to pay. Wrapped in content clothing, someone else pays you to publish your content. Quality is of little importance.

Let's say you fancy setting up a music TV channel. Not altogether an original idea, it's almost a commodity market. A generation on from the 1980s when MTV pioneered the format, a glut of channels now caters for narrower music genres, broadcasting endless videos interrupted only by advertising. Perhaps now is the time for an entrepreneurial channel to emerge and steal the audience?

Your research for, say, a new karaoke channel reveals that enough people want to be pop stars that they're prepared to make their own demo videos, almost all of questionable quality, but that they will willingly pay to see broadcast. Aspiring pop stars can tell their friends when their video is due to be aired, alert their local paper, and inform prospective agents that a new hit artist is up for grabs. If it costs £500,000 to hire airtime for a year, and there are 105,000 blocks of five minutes, then £5 per nightmare karaoke would turn a profit. And surely with a sparkling career worth millions at stake, people would pay much more than that? The fact that there is no discernable audience, nor advertisers who would want to touch it, need not matter. Your business is as a distribution intermediary, more than it is in content production, and that is a safer business than trying to create transferable hits.

Not that it's completely risk-free. MTV is an intermediary as well as a content brand, suffering the schizophrenic middle ground between content provider and distributor (but coping admirably and profitably). While it needs a distribution mechanism itself to get into homes, it is an intermediary for other people's content – music videos. That same content is also broadcast by other aggregators, making differentiation dependent on branding, scheduling and live programme production. MTV produces many hours of proprietary content, for a cooler, newsier, youth-oriented feel. But original content is more expensive and riskier to produce than other people's videos, putting pressure on margins. Power then moves further towards distributors as carriage fees – the money distributors pay to some channels – come under pressure. Distributors don't necessarily want to spend money on highly commoditized video channels, and neither do they want to pay broadcasters excessive premium rates for aggregated content that they can get cheaper elsewhere. If you want to make money and it comes to a choice between producing content and being a distributor (providing you have masses of capital to invest), then be a distributor.

THE CHANGING VALUE CHAIN

Distributors of old enjoyed a simple life, whether they originated their own content or bought it in. Supply being limited, audiences would turn up to consume whatever was on offer and, providing the costs of the content plus distribution were lower than revenues from customers, profit rolled in. British commercial television, a heavily regulated monopoly supplier of advertising up to the 1990s, used to be a licence to print money.

The distribution value chain was blown apart by the digital transformation, affecting old media as much as the new. New television channels take to the air as bandwidth becomes cheap. More books, a medium once said to be under threat as everyone took to reading novels on handheld devices, are published each year. Booksellers, virtual and real, flourish. If you make music, then it can be published as a digital file and distributed through any number of Web aggregators without the need for a recording contract. Of course, without the recording contract, the big book deal, and the distribution of your TV content on a big channel, your content may not just be not sticky: it may not be noticed in the first place.

Responding to technological change, established distributors made up strategy as they went along. Doing something is usually better than doing nothing.

Which is why newspaper groups, at first dismissive of the Internet (one editor rightly claimed that the Web isn't easy to tuck under your arm or read on the train, and performs less well than a paper when someone spills coffee on it), eventually pumped hundreds of millions of dollars into online ventures. Despite the dotcom euphoria, it wasn't an easy time to make investments of such magnitude. During the 1990s, newspaper circulation fell. In the UK, the combined sales of national daily and Sunday newspapers dropped by 8%. Not since the advent of broadcasting had any major new distributive threat visited itself upon the news market. After a start in which most papers simply published online versions of their print products, adept publishing groups transformed their digital content, bought in new expertise, and built strong new media properties to complement – not cannibalize – their newspapers. It cost a lot of money.

Newspaper and magazine publishers are conservative businesses, many with histories extending back a century or more. During the lifetime of some employees not yet in their thirties, journalists' copy used to be rekeyed by unionized typesetters and pages cast in hot metal. Newspaper groups are not the quickest businesses to adapt to change. In trying, some started enterprises at an arm's length from their existing, proven business, which at least enjoy established audience loyalties. Others chose what they took to be a cool path in the transition to digital distribution – starting subsidiaries with whacky names, fun working environments, and little contact with the parent business. The best, most commendably the *New York Times* and the *Wall Street Journal*, transferred existing customers online by offering interactive content under their established brand names. Similar content, similar brand, similar audience – a simple way to improve the chances of transferring hit content.

WHEN BIG IS BEAUTIFUL

Distribution power is largely consolidated in global businesses, competing for hit content from providers they know will deliver audiences to their platforms. The biggest global distributors are also producers or content commissioners, and there has been a flurry of merger activity to build integrated businesses.

Time Warner, magazine and music publisher, and owner of legendary film studio Warner Brothers, was already a creative giant when in 1999 it took the hand (and, in the new tradition of the dotcom era, $106 billion of highly valued paper, cash not seeming important at the time) of AOL to form the world's most formidable new and old media combinations.

With size comes synergy – the money to do further deals and buy the world's most attractive, addictive content, such as the Harry Potter franchise, which the group successfully exploited across its businesses. Large corporations also attract talent, which sees substantial budgets being made available for the creation of big, transferable stories that build hit properties. Leveraging talent, craft skills, massive distribution capabilities, its world-beating entertainment brands, and access to financial markets, there is no distribution conundrum for Time Warner AOL (only one of shareholder value). Small isn't an issue. Big is beautiful.

Because technology doesn't recognize national boundaries, companies defined by their nationality or regionality are organizations under threat – or at least destined to remain small. Big distributors are predators. There's little room for Mister In-between. The choice is between finding a profitable niche and being one of the biggest guns in the battalion, or a continuing struggle to make ends meet.

Distribution, being financially more rewarding than content creation, leads distributors to chase larger market shares. Domestic legislators may hate it, seeing consolidation as a cultural threat to national identity, but many small, home-grown media businesses are facing the end of independence.

At the same time, regulators, naturally reluctant to deregulate themselves out of a job, are moving only slowly to abandon introspective, nationalistic rules. Even as late as 2002, the law prevented the UK's main commercial television station being owned by a single company. And until the 1980s, the septuagenarian FCC, which regulates US broadcasting, had a seven-station rule – no one company could own more than seven radio or TV stations. The number was eventually raised to 12, provided they reach no more than 25% of the national audience. Similar rules in Europe are frequently based on the share of national advertising spend. So the more successful a distributor becomes, and the more the audience wants to spend time with them, the closer they are to breaking the rules. With a regulated limit on success beyond which companies are penalized, growth comes more easily from a multi-market strategy, building a series of maximum-share businesses in many countries.

TALENT COSTS MORE IN CROWDED MARKETS

Distribution economics, turned on its head from the times when manufacturing and storage were costly links in the chain, means audiences should pay less for content. Supply outstrips demand. But the supply-demand equilibrium is compounded by talent inflation and an ability to create (combined with the demand to consume) ever bigger stories. Bigger productions with big talent cost bigger bucks, and the biggest bucks are found within giant companies. That gives talent a leverage to demand more pampering, largely in the form of money, and also provides an incentive for distributors and content producers to pamper all the more.

When Disney/ABC contemplated dumping its highly respected but lower-rating news show *Nightline* to court chat-show host David Letterman, the presenter eventually found himself keeping the same job with the same network, but with a substantial fillip both to his personal fee and that paid to his production company, a total of $70 million a year. Only the biggest media companies can afford that kind of money, and trying to recoup it through advertising slots and global syndication is a risky game. Mariah Carey received £38 million *not* to make music for EMI, the result of paying up her contract when album sales failed to materialize. Humble authors find stories they have yet to write commanding awesome advances. Even history professors, cooks or decorators can, with the right spit and polish, find celebrity to be a lucrative profession, with TV shows, books, videos and syndicated Web content providing nice little earners. Talent that becomes a brand becomes expensive, even – and here's the rub – when the talent has more ambition than talent and is simply a creation of the distributor's own making. The demand for branded talent – that with which the audience already identifies because of existing distribution – leads to a spiralling escalation of its costs.

But it is an escalation from which producers can profit – if they have talent contracted to them with whom audiences want to spend time. When content attracts audiences to distribution platforms, or encourages them to stay longer, then distributors and content aggregators will pay. Sport is one of the stickiest magnets for audiences, causing the value of sports rights to soar – to the point where some distributors find it difficult to make their rights acquisitions pay. In Germany, the Kirsch Group bought broadcast rights to the 2002 soccer world cup and then couldn't recoup the fee by selling on rights to individual television markets. Although it was not due entirely to the football rights issue, this was a critical factor, and Kirsch went kaput before a world cup ball was kicked.

CONSUMPTION IS CHEAP

On the Web, the audience's expectation is that only a very limited amount of content has a value for which they will pay. The rest should be free or at least very, very cheap. It is a reflection of the economics of mass media with which most people have been brought up. Records, newspapers, books are all relatively cheap. The marginal cost of adding another viewer to broadcast television is almost nothing. The cost of seeing a film, which may have cost more than $100 million to produce, is a few dollars if one wants to see it early. When it costs almost the same to distribute 20 million copies of a song over the Internet as it does just one, audiences feel cheated if some of the savings are not passed on. Premium content has, to date, been limited to porn, movies and sport and, to a lesser extent, exclusive business information.

New media has made audiences less reluctant to pay for content, not more, with a resulting impact on the economics of old methods of distribution. For example, worldwide CD sales were absolutely flat for the last five years of the 1990s, before taking a double-digit dive in the first two years of the millennium. But audiences still listen to music as much as ever – they just don't buy as many CDs. The Record Industry Association of America says that almost one-quarter of consumers don't get their music from shops any more, preferring free downloads from the Internet.

It's nothing new. Paying for content has never been universal. Although almost everyone listens to music in some form at some time – on the radio, in bars, at work – about 90% of people never buy it. The industry's response to blank cassette sales in the 1970s was the outraged claim that 'home taping is killing music', and although the words may be different today the message is the same. Record labels fear that free distribution will push the 90% non-purchasing population closer to 100%. As margins are tight enough already, there's little point them remaining in business.

Vivendi Universal's former CEO, Jean-Marie Messier, whose empire included a major music business, predicted that most people will download music from the Web on to mobile phones, where it will remain until needed. It need not be free, providing consumers don't feel they're being ripped off. Managed properly, the music industry's revenues could double within five years, from $40 billion in 2001 to $90 billion.

That's despite the fact that music download websites, many purveying material for which they do not own the rights, continue to put pressure on the margins of established distributors. Piracy of the old-fashioned, hard-copy sort, evidenced by an increase in prosecutions of CD bootleggers and rogue traders, keeps on rising. There's a market for dodgy goods, especially as digital reproduction makes copies that are almost perfect for a fraction of the price in the shops. The combined number of illegal downloads and pirated CDs is not small – more than one-third of CDs and audio cassettes on the planet are pirated copies according to the International Federation of the Phonographic Industry (which needs a name change if it's to sound even remotely like it's heard of the Internet). While sales of genuine recorded music have been on a downward trajectory, sales of recordable blank CDs have shot through the roof – five billion were sold in 2001, making them the fastest growing pirate format. It's an equal and opposite reaction that causes furrowed brows among rights owners and is big business in emerging markets. If you want to get rich as a DVD pirate, China is the place to be. With the number of western films that can be released officially in the republic restricted to 12 a year, Hollywood block-busters are in particular demand.

The IFPI claims that about half of all recordable CDs are used for illegal reproduction of copyright material. So the market for pirate music CDs is the same size as legitimate sales. With much music being bought by young, IT-literate consumers who are generally uninterested in the finer details of copyright law, record companies have to find new ways of distributing music – to the satisfaction not just of buyers but of their artists too. Musicians also have more control in the digital world, having found independent labels that use online aggregators to distribute music, or even creating markets of their own. Unsigned artists in particular can bypass distributors if they wish. They may need big distribution if they want to be big stars, but one no longer needs a contract with a major label to get one's music heard. Once major established recording artists decide they no longer need record labels, more customers will find a need to use, and pay for, downloads.

Like perfume and apparel brands, record companies see piracy as a threat to sales and reputation, not a promotional opportunity. It is something to be stopped. But in restricting illegal distribution, much of it appreciated by audiences – some of whom can reasonably be expected to buy content legally too – distributors look like corporate killjoys protecting their fiefdoms. Few people who use Web or broadband music content are criminals, and wise businesspeople don't treat customers like thieves. Better to find ways to make the illegal legal. The five major record companies control 80% of the global record business, so distribution is something they are unlikely to give up lightly. Ultimate control, though, has gone forever.

The industry would deny they are killjoys, admitting only that they take action to protect their investments. So, for example, music major EMI says it acts on behalf of artists and composers when it prevents suppliers of mobile phone ringtones from using their music. Here is a service in heavy demand, for which there are millions of customers who have shown a willingness to pay for new ringtones, which they change frequently. It's a promotional opportunity as well as a revenue-generating one. A gift horse. With the introduction of the ringtone charts comes additional publicity – and the incentive to rise up the chart. However, that's not the way some music companies want their property promoted, even though composers could actually earn more royalties. Then again, when you've written a great tune, you may prefer it to be performed by a respected orchestra, not a mobile phone.

HOOKING THE AUDIENCE IN THE ATTENTION-BASED ECONOMY

Distributors and producers should have the perfect marriage. Distributors require a constant stream of high-quality content that attracts subscribers and advertisers and keeps audiences loyal to their platforms. Producers seek distribution in high-profile places where audiences gather. Both want to create the hit property, not just the hit.

When they work together to promote content across media, even dodgy stories can attract a sizable audience which transfers. The *Blair Witch Project* was hyped first on the Web, purporting to be the scariest movie ever. Eventually, it grossed $240 million and became one of the top 150 films ever made (measured by value, not critical acclaim). But the hype created expectations that the production couldn't meet, leaving much of the audience disappointed: 85% of people chose not to go back for the second instalment, and its sequel, *Book of Shadows*, grossed less than $40 million. *Blair Witch*, a case study in the use of the Internet as a marketing, community and content tool in movies, fooled the audience only once. Die-hard fans, however, still enjoy a thriving Blair Witch community on the Web.

We have moved from a distribution-based economy – where if content got carriage it got consumed – into an attention-based economy, where the objective is to take a share of the audience's time. No matter how good it is – and there is some very good content that doesn't get the audience it deserves – content has to stand out to achieve longevity and transferability. Audiences no longer passively consume anything put before them. They are active decision-makers, media-savvy, making positive choices from an avalanche of content. Time is too short to waste it on indifferent, poorly told stories.

This is the first generation of content decision-makers, and it costs a lot of money to turn their heads. Marketing a Hollywood blockbuster can easily cost as much as making the movie in the first place. It requires further promotion as it passes through the distribution chain, into video rental, video sales, and the sale of broadcast rights to pay television and eventually free-to-air television.

The Internet may be perceived as a cheap option, but websites that are not promoted simply don't get seen. Anyone can put up a website, but no one will come. Integrated marketing programmes, across the Web, traditional media advertising, and sales promotions benefit from synergy and may be worth more than the sum of the parts. But all those parts are all pretty expensive. Getting noticed costs money.

Grabbing attention by standing out from all other content, presenting a compelling reason for the audience to spend time with the distributor, is the aim.

- Start early. Put up that website, even though no one will come without promotion for it. Get it properly meta-tagged and listed on Web directories.

- Make it professional. Audiences can be fooled once by the deliberately amateur approach, but this is a competitive market where professionaliam pays. Not too many people went back to see *Blair Witch Project 2*.

- Tell enough of the target market that your content is there. Viral marketing programmes and word of mouth all help.

- Provide a clear benefit that audiences want to hear. Tell a story about the story.

- Tell the story in other media. Audiences become loyal to content and stories, not the delivery mechanism.

- Find attention-building partners – those who can cross-promote, or who have a sticky audience of their own.

- Enlist the help of important intermediaries, particularly content aggregators and digital guides.

Distributors seek addictive content for the obvious reason that it encourages consumers to spend time – and usually more money – with them. While the audience is hooked, they find it hard to transfer their allegiances.

Packaging creative content to make sticky schedules, or transfering the audience through different media in a package, is an art form in transition.

Finding content that commands attention can form a base from which to package newer, less well-known, or even weaker content, so building a bigger audience. In television terms, this is 'hammocking', protecting new content with 'bankers' to which audiences seem guaranteed to come. Once caught up in the first piece of content, the theory is that passivity prevents people switching away from the second – they would have to make such an effort to return for the other key show a short while later. Networks used to win whole evenings of viewing in this way. In the new world, it's harder to protect slots, and schedules are disappearing as personal television recorders select favoured material on behalf of their owners. Marketing content becomes more important than scheduling.

Packaging creative content to make sticky schedules, or transfering the audience through different media in a package, is an art form in transition. Like the old marketing adage that it is less costly to retain an existing customer than it is to recruit a new one, so is it easier to encourage an audience to stay with an existing piece of content than it is to sell something entirely new. New niche channels are able to command some kind of audience if they buy in hit content from existing channels.

With the audience fragmenting, choosing to dip in and out of distribution channels quickly, just in time to get to the content they know and bypassing the rest, it's getting harder to cross-promote new content. Forrester Research estimates that by 2006, 40% of television viewing will be on-demand – that is, not part of general grazing or zapping. Audiences increasingly access content from electronic programme guides, personalized to tune in or record programmes automatically. If they wished, distributors could charge for a higher profile on the EPG, or even for recommending new content to subscribers. 'If you liked this film, you're bound to appreciate this new TV series …' It's the televisual equivalent of high-street booksellers charging publishers to move books up the bestsellers list – and thus making titles appear to be a must-read. These are the charts that give the appearance of independence – but are far from such.

LOYALTY BIG AND SMALL

Niche audiences, those who come together exclusively to participate in a shared interest, have a high rate of loyalty to their interest, but not necessarily the medium in which they consume it. Anyone providing content in new ways can open up opportunities to transfer across media. Fresh-water anglers watch fishing programmes, visit angling websites, and buy *Salmon Monthly* magazine. They are not simply hooked on to a single medium that fulfils every fishing fantasy. Great content, preferably better than anyone else's, will attract a following among the addicted, who may also be prepared to pay.

At their most potent, niches incite passion and build communities. Niche audiences are more enthusiastic than general ones, with a greater inclination to spend money on new content and related material. Fanatics may be relatively small in number, but they tend to stick around for longer. And they come back.

Like people who are particularly wedded to rather obscure religions, audiences for niche content are evangelical, spreading the good word and trying to convert anyone polite enough to show an interest. They will capture a few, put off many more, but if the recruits turn out to be as sticky as the missionaries, then they can be profitable. True niche audiences are loyal. They're sticky. Conversely, the broader the content, the more mainstream the audience, and the more take-it-or-leave-it they become – except to the biggest pieces of content, with the biggest talents, telling the biggest stories. They are sticky too. Mainstream audiences bring revenues through sheer size.

Esoteric content targeted at a tiny, specialized audience in a single medium has a limit to the revenues it can achieve. Few low-budget pieces of content become worldwide hits. When they do, they get talked about, generating more interest, bigger audiences, greater profit. They are exceptions. Small audiences generally mean small revenues – even if cost per acquisition is low and associated income high. Big stories for a worldwide market, delivered across many media, each medium fulfilling a different part of the story, has a much greater profit potential.

But when audiences fragment without creating identifiable niches of people with common interests, the result is just a lot of small audiences, consuming lots of different types of content for not particularly lengthy periods of time. They are loyal neither to the content nor the medium, and prove problematic to providers of general interest content who are not leaders in their fields. Not only do these pieces of content or channels achieve low market share, being chosen by fewer people, they are also chosen less loyally by those people. (The opposite of the niche pattern, it also counters the loyalty achieved by mass distribution channels. The same phenomenon, according to Professor Patrick Barwise of London Business School, also occurs with branded goods. It's called double jeopardy.) The strength of the link between audience size and loyalty depends on the medium and the type of content. It is generally stronger for pull media, such as the Internet, where audiences make active decisions to visit particular sites, than it is for 'push' media, such as television, where people are more likely to graze whatever is on. On the Web, larger branded sites attract the most loyal audiences. As more content comes online, the stronger this association – audiences rely on channels and content they know best, either because of the brand name, or because they reflect their own particular interests.

- Big hits need big distribution: if you want a small, intimate audience, fine. But it results in small revenues, which affects your ability to tell a big story.
- Hook audiences early – a strong first hit is important (your Web home page, hit single, big movie).
- Put more resources into your opening offer if you can.
- Invest in talent.
- Build a flagship.
- Work stories across media – transferability.
- Develop new ones at the same time.
- Niche audiences, being evangelical, can transfer to other media.
- Niche usually means small – but one can attract a premium for content that is in demand by small groups of evangelists.
- Fragmenting mainstream audiences are not niches – simply small groups splitting their time between lots of content and spreading revenues thinly.

MAKING IT ALL PAY

So you have a story to tell, a piece of content with power to last a few years, transfer across media, and create self-perpetuating communities who pass the story along. Starting the ball rolling is going to be costly, but with audiences expected to hammer at the door for your content, a comfortable, early retirement is within your reach. Perfect.

Creative risks aside, the financial challenge is one that is common to any business – achieving a decent return on one's investment. Raising capital – usually substantial – managing costs, hiring talent, sourcing materials, and then turning out a product that people want to buy. If a sizable target market buys it once, then it's a hit. When they return for more, it's a hit property. The franchise.

Hits, though, are fickle things. No matter how thorough the research, content can miss its mark, with dire financial consequences. Making a business out of hit properties requires investors with nerves of steel. You need a strong constitution to hold on to sports stocks, for example, where a couple of poor scores could take your club out of a tournament and kill subsequent revenues from ticket sales, merchandise and broadcast rights.

Creative business relies on cross-subsidization – production of the many dependent on the success of the few. The hit content business is the miss business too – and misses are considerably more prevalent than hits. Developing portfolios of content is a method of risk management by which sticky hits pay for the more frequent disappointments. When a single film can wipe out a studio's profits for the year (or provide a substantial bonanza that will generate revenues for many years to come), when a single hit album may have to pay for a couple of hundred losers, and when a tiny number of bestsellers have to keep a publishing house afloat, that's sticky risky business. A record released on a major label has to sell about half a million copies worldwide to break even. In 2001, just 112 albums from a total of 6,500 released by US majors sold as many. That's under 2% of records breaking even. The hits business is tough. Yet the music business still gets a bad press for exploiting artists and fans.

With misses outnumbering hits, forecasting likely revenues is less an exact science than a finger-in-the-air estimate. Creative businesses may like to suggest otherwise, but the reality is that until the content hits the marketplace, no one really knows what is going to work and what isn't. No one sets out deliberately to make mediocre content, it just happens that way. Most content loses money because it's so hard to do well.

Unlike traditional business planning, where costs are planned against likely future revenue targets, producing content is inherently riskier. The numbers are based on assumptions of the likely market size, competitive activity, and so forth, but figures for the strength of content can't be tested as easily. Management of content businesses is an art form as much as the content creation itself – requiring people to deliver strategy without the assuredness that one piece of output will be very similar to the next. Creative talent and creative *management* talent may be a surer indicator of future success than a rock solid business plan, full of numbers, but light on creative rationale. Financial analysis, whilst important, at some stage has to give way to instinct. The content business is a creative business, and sometimes the financial guys have to hold their tongues and go with the flow.

'Information wants to be free', according to net guru Stewart Brand. Even if information wants to be, it's certainly not in the interests of content producers for it to be so. Customers understandably prefer not to pay, which is the fault of early Internet pioneers encouraging consumers to expect something for nothing. All in the interests of building market share and hoping that enough people would become addicted enough that they would be happy to pay in the future.

Audiences have become so used to going online for only the modest costs of connection, and to sites that may require a few personal details by way of an entry fee, that the economic omens for creative content producers on the Web are pretty bleak. Quality content costs money to produce – money that may not be easily recouped through advertising, sponsorship or customer fees. Customers don't want to pay, and audiences are too fragmented or unattractive for advertisers to buy space.

Free Web content puts pressure on prices in other media. Customers get so used to not paying for some content that they expect not to pay for much at all – unless it is perceived to be 'premium' (very, very new, or very scarce). In print, even the hundreds of pages of content of the *New York Times* and the UK's *Sunday Times* come for the price of a cup of coffee. When advertising revenues dip and publishers try to recover some profits through price-rises, customers resist. Sales generally drop – and advertising income falls correspondingly. Margins in some publishing businesses are under such pressure that it can actually cost more to produce the periodical than can be recovered from a sale. Publishers can try to make their package more attractive, with specialist sections for gardening, money, motoring, holidays and property in the hope that advertising will make up for the loss incurred in making the publication stronger. In this way, classified advertising subsidizes print, but if advertising dries up, so do profits.

Prospects are brighter in the fragmented games industry, which has successfully extracted revenues from addicts. Here, consumers have been prepared to pay £40 or more for a new piece of software. With new games consoles Web connected, players are on the brink of paying monthly fees to do battle with other players.

Cheap Web content in entertainment and news will eventually become poor Internet content, with only the most popular generating sufficient advertising. Specialized sites, such as the *Wall Street Journal* in business news, may be able to charge subscriptions and attract a premium, if relatively small, audience. More consumers will have to get used to putting their hands in their pockets more often.

But audiences will only pick up the bill if they believe content to be truly valuable. Content needs to be enjoyable or worthwhile, delivered faster and looking the high-tech part. Jerky downloads and frequent crashes, acceptable but irritating when the content is free, won't be tolerated by paying customers. Audiences consume content, not technology, and are understandably frustrated when enjoyment is curtailed because of IT problems outside their control. When the meter is running, customers feel cheated when the promise is broken.

When digital television launched in 1999, at a cost of about £30 a month for a full subscription package, British homes could suddenly receive between 20 and 200 channels – a substantial jump from the standard five terrestrial stations. But some consumers who tried watching TV during heavy rain found their picture pixellating. Service suspended and rain stopped play. The new, digital technology – a string of ones and zeros bouncing off a satellite or through an existing aerial – didn't always work in a downpour. When people are paying considerable sums of discretionary income on services they previously would have gone without, they expect a decent return. At the very least, they expect it to work. Most people accept that Internet sites are slow, and sometimes unavailable, which is tolerable when they are free and plenty of alternatives exist. Consumers can always choose never to visit again. Choices are harder when people are tied into ongoing subscriptions.

But audiences have proved willing to pay for new forms of content, which, on the face of it, may appear of little relevance to anyone – tiny, dot-matrix games on mobile phone interfaces and ringtones, for example, or the average £400 per year per subscriber to interactive television platforms. Quality, being in the eyes of the beholder, is either niche content – small audiences happy to consume content of personal interest to them, regardless of the production values (it's the story that counts) – or the biggest productions, attracting the largest audiences and the biggest talents. The two ends of the continuum are where profits reside – providing the story is strong.

EPILOGUE

When Mr Gutenberg knocked together his printing press, its biggest impact was on education, democratizing reading and learning. But it also formed a new creative outlet for the sharing of stories. In time, the novel became a dominant art form, as important to the culture of the nine-teenth century as the theatre was to England in the sixteenth century.

Then, a little over 100 years ago, on 12 December 1901, Guglielmo Marconi flew a kite off the coast of Newfoundland and from it trailed an aerial. Soon, the Morse code letter 'S' was being picked up by the aerial from a transmission base on the Isle of Wight, more than 2,000 miles away. This, the original wireless, although a significant technological achievement, was hardly rich in content, the letter 'S' being hard pressed to command an appreciative audience week in, week out. In the absence of compelling content, Marconi's transmission of Morse code would remain a party trick, a piece of technology redundant in the days before Oprah Winfrey and *Pick of the Pops*. Radio waves needed news, quizzes, soap operas and chat shows to fulfill their creative potential. Creative con-tent makes technology purposeful.

Now, newer technologies personalize content and reduce shared expe-riences. The one-to-many paradigm of book to readers, TV show to viewers, CD to listeners, is not at an end. But it is an aging business model in the process of adaptation. The future will not be broad, but if possible won't be exclusively narrow either. This is the multiband world. One in which the digitally connected already receive more than 200 television channels yet choose to watch very few of them. Where consumers can access millions of websites but rely upon the same old dozen.

The challenge for those with a story to tell is to build content that becomes a favourite – by creating content across many media, fitting the right elements of the story to the right medium. Transfer and adapt. Strong stories, well told, which transfer, and which are told in the right medium, can become addictive. Making it is hard to do. With much mediocre content in every medium every day, consumers seek out the very best. Material they know they can trust. They are even prepared to pay. That's good news for people who tell stories. Content creators crave audience – the biggest one possible for their art. They demand to be read, seen and heard. To share their stories and make a business out of imagination.

Yet content that engages with even the largest audiences can still fail the test of time. But the biggest stories extend across media and down generations, adapting to new media, remaining comfortable with the old. It may stand tall in the medium for which it was originally produced, yet still work and be appreciated elsewhere.

The mantra that content is king is just a saying, just jargon. Audiences really demand quality, sticky, addictive content; stories that transfer and endure. When they find wonderful content, they want it to go on and on and on. To paraphrase Hemingway, a great story is like an iceberg. One-eighth is told in one place, the rest is found elsewhere.

We will shortly enter the second decade of new-media content creation, long enough for aesthetic conventions to have been established. A website looks like this, and a text message like that. Conventions of traditional media have not been abandoned. Audiences still understand what a movie looks like – it's usually somewhere between 90 and 150 minutes long, generally has three acts (the beginning, middle and end), and appears first in a cinema, then on video, and eventually ends up on television. If you want to see the content early, you have to make an effort, go into town and pay for it. Then, as time goes by, it becomes easier and cheaper to access. Audiences understand their role within the conventions of media. They appreciate the relationship between time and cost. And they demand value for their money, and the giving of their time.

New devices haven't changed existing conventions for old media much. But they do create new ways for stories to be told. Technology hasn't reinvented film-making, music-making, or the news. But it has allowed content creators to capture bigger audiences faster. And tell stories in new ways.

Read the news and reviews columns and it would be tempting to believe high standards are behind us. That the plethora of content inevitably means most is poor. It is true that much is, and always has been. For creativity is a risky business where quality hits are but a fraction of the whole. Novelist Kingsley Amis declared that 'more means worse', and there are many who would agree with him. But more means more of the better too. More for audiences to select content that is right for them.

But 'more' is a concept related to distribution, not quality. And for most in the audience, distribution is irrelevant beyond the basis question of cost. More important is the attention that creative businesses pay to the development of enjoyable content, which audiences want to consume. More can mean better. Whatever new media arise.

FURTHER READING

MUSIC

Hit Men by Fredric Dannen (Vintage Books, 1991) is a colourful analysis of the music business.

BROADCASTING

For an entertaining look at how a policy of driving down ratings to build credibility can pay off, try *The Nation's Favourite: the true adventures of Radio 1*, by Simon Garfield (Faber and Faber, 1998).

More seriously, *A Social History of British Broadcasting* by Paddy Scannell and David Cardiff (Basil Blackwell, 1991) provides a comprehensive account of the development of policy, programmes and personalities.

Dished: the rise and fall of British satellite broadcasting, by Peter Chippendale and Suzanne Franks (Simon & Schuster, 1991), provides a romping case study of how concentrating on technology rather than content can lead to disaster.

Ownership battles of American networks and the damage caused by new delivery systems are covered in *Three Blind Mice: how the TV networks lost their way*, by Ken Auletta (Vintage Books, 1992).

Definitions of audience, research methodologies and a quality versus popularity examination in *Desperately Seeking the Audience* by Ien Ang (Routledge, 1991).

With a section on stickiness in television content, read *The Tipping Point* by Malcolm Gladwell (Little, Brown, 2000).

FILM

From Script to Screen: the collaborative art of filmmaking, by Linda Seger and Edward Jay Whetmore (Henry Holt, 1994).

INTERACTIVE MEDIA

Writing for Interactive Media, by Jon Samsel and Darryl Wimberley (Allworth Press, 1998) is a detailed how-to-do-it guide to storytelling in non-linear environments.

Building portfolio businesses in the new media world is covered in *The Monk and the Riddle*, by Randy Komisar with Kent Lineback (Harvard Business School Press, 2000).

NEWS

Old, but worth a look, is Edward Jay Epstein's *News from Nowhere* (Ivan R. Dee, 1965, reissued 2000).

How ratings determine what gets on air as competition intensifies is covered in *Downsizing the News*, by Penn Kimball (Woodrow Wilson Centre Press, 1994).

FAIRY TALES

The definitive guide to the history and interpretation of fairy tales in *The Uses of Enchantment: the meaning and importance of fairy tales*, by Bruno Bettelheim (Penguin, 1976).

INDEX

Simply Brilliant
Fergus O'Connell
0273 654187

The world is full of smart, experienced, skilled, brilliant people. However, many people – even smart ones – are lacking a set of essential skills that when pulled together can be termed 'common sense'. This book provides a set of principles to make the bright better.

Marketing Judo
John Barnes & Richard Richardson
0273 66316X

How to build your business through brilliant marketing – but without a big budget. As in judo, use your brains not brawn, and leverage the weight of your opponent to your advantage. Written by two men who did just that, to make Harry Ramsden's into a multi-million pound business.

Weak at the Top
0273 656821

Monday
Recruitment week! This is where I play God and toy with other people's lives…

Tuesday
Working from gym today. Told Hayley I need to spend more time looking at the figures. Have diverted all calls to our Customer Careline…

Wednesday
Got in so late I hardly had time to bin post, delete e-mails and cancel meetings before lunch…

John Weak
You don't want to work with him.
You certainly don't want to be him.
But you sure as hell want to read him.

Please visit our website at:
www.business-minds.com